The Psalms

Poetry on Fire

Translated from Hebrew Text

DR. BRIAN SIMMONS

BroadStreet
PUBLISHING

The Psalms: Poetry on Fire, The Passion Translation®
Translated directly from the original Hebrew text by Dr. Brian Simmons

Published by BroadStreet Publishing Group, LLC
Racine, Wisconsin, USA
www.broadstreetpublishing.com

ISBN-13: 9781424549368 (paperback)
ISBN-13: 9781424549740 (e-book)

Cover and interior design by Garborg Design Works, Inc. | www.garborgdesign.com
Interior typesetting by Katherine Lloyd | www.theDESKonline.com

Printed in the United States of America

Translator's Introduction

I have loved the Psalms for over forty years. They have been my comfort and joy, leading me to the place where worship flows. When discouraged or downcast, I have never failed to take new strength from reading the Psalms. They charge my batteries and fill my sails. In fact, they seem to grow even more powerful as I grow older. Their thunder stirs me; their sweet melodies move me into the sacred emotions of a heart on fire. The dark rain clouds of grief turn to bright rainbows of hope, just from meditating on David's soul-subduing songs.

The Psalms find the words that express our deepest and strongest emotions, no matter what the circumstances. Every emotion of our hearts is reflected in the Psalms. Reading the Psalms will turn sighing into singing and trouble into triumph. The word *praise* is found 189 times in this book. There is simply nothing that touches my heart like the Psalms. Thousands of years ago my deepest feelings were put to music—this is what we all delightfully discover when reading the Psalms!

Poetry on Fire

The Psalms are clearly poetic. They are praises placed inside of poetry. Everyone who reads the Psalms realizes how filled with emotion they are! You will never be bored in reading the poetry that spills out of a fiery, passionate heart. These verses contain both poetry and music that touch the heart deeply. Much of Christianity has become so intellectualized that our emotions and artistic creativity are often set aside as unimportant in the worship of God. The Psalms free us to become emotional, passionate, sincere worshippers. It is time to sing the Psalms! For this reason, I believe a contemporary name for the book of Psalms could be—Poetry on Fire! These 150 poetic masterpieces give us an expression of faith and worship. They become a mirror to the heart of God's people in our quest to experience God's presence.

The Psalms are pure praise, inspired by the breath of God. Praise is a matter of life and breath. As long as we have breath we are told to praise the Lord. The Psalms release an anointing of praise that will lift heaviness off the human heart.

The Psalms are meant to do to you what they did to David. They will bring you from your cave of despair into the glad presence of the King who likes you the way you are.

The Psalms are prayers. The Psalms have been called the "little brother" of prayer. Mixed with intercession, the Psalms become the fuel for our devotional life. Each psalm is a prayer. The early church recited and sang the Psalms regularly. So many contemporary worship songs have been inspired by this book of prayer-poetry!

The Psalms will unlock mysteries and parables, for in the purest praise is the cryptic language of a prophet. The wisdom of God is contained in these 150 keys. You have a key chain with master keys to unlock God's storehouse of wisdom and revelation. It is the "harp" (anointed worship) that releases divine secrets. Read carefully Psalm 49:4 tpt: "I will break open mysteries with my music and my song will release riddles solved."

The prophetic anointing rests upon the Psalms. David's harp will bring revelation and understanding to the people. Singers who tap into the anointing of the Psalms will bring forth truths in their songs that will break the hearts of people and release divine understanding to the church. The prophets must become musicians, and the musicians must become prophets for the key of David to be given to the church.

How Are the Psalms Divided?

The Psalms are really five books in one. Moses gave us the five books of the Law called the Pentateuch; David gives us the five books of the Psalms. Each division ends with a doxology that includes the words, "Amen and Amen." The last division ends with Psalm 150 as the doxology, forming an appropriate conclusion to this "Pentateuch of David." These five divisions have been compared to the first five books of the Bible:

Book I	Psalms 1–41 (Genesis) Psalms of man and creation.
Book II	Psalms 42–72 (Exodus) Psalms of suffering and redemption.
Book III	Psalms 73–89 (Leviticus) Psalms of worship and God's house.
Book IV	Psalms 90–106 (Numbers) Psalms of our pilgrimage on earth.
Book V	Psalms 107–150 (Deuteronomy) Psalms of praise and the Word.

Christ in the Psalms

The Psalms are all about Jesus Christ. There are 150 Psalms and each of them reveals a special and unique aspect of the God-Man, Christ Jesus. Every Psalm is messianic in that they all point to our Lord Jesus, whom God has chosen as King over all. The Psalms find their fulfillment in Christ. These songs are all about Jesus. The key to understanding the Psalms is to look for Jesus within its pages. Luke 24:44 tpt says: "This is what I told you while I was still with you: Everything must be fulfilled that is written about me in the Law of Moses, the Prophets and the *Psalms*." There are many secrets about Jesus waiting to be discovered here!

A Word about The Passion Translation

Bible translations are both a gift and a problem. They give us the words God spoke through his servants, but words can become very poor containers for revelation. They leak! Over time the words change from one generation to the next. Meaning is influenced by culture, background, and a thousand other details. You can imagine how differently the Hebrew authors of the Old Testament saw the world from three thousand years ago!

There is no such thing as a truly literal translation of the Bible, for there is not an equivalent language that perfectly conveys the meaning of the text except as it is understood in its original cultural and linguistic setting. Therefore, a translation can be a problem. The problem, however, is solved when we seek to transfer meaning, and not merely words, from the original text to the receptor language.

To transfer meaning from one language to another, as it relates to the Bible narrative, requires interpretation. Every translation, sadly, interposes a fallible human interpretation between the reader and an infallible text. At times, after much textual research, I was simply forced to interpret the text and carry over its meaning so that contemporary English speakers would be able to comprehend it and receive its impact. Undoubtedly, this cannot be considered a perfect science, but more of an artistic, Spirit-led production. I have sought to do my best to bring the meaning over from Hebrew into modern English, along with the poetic nuances that will make it sparkle and come alive to the reader.

So without further introduction, I present to you—Poetry on Fire! And may the Holy Spirit fill you with joy and revelation as you read it!

—Dr. Brian Simmons

BOOK I

The "Genesis" Psalms

PSALMS OF MAN AND CREATION

Psalm 1

THE TREE OF LIFE[a]

1What delight comes to those[b]
Who follow God's ways!
They won't walk in step with the wicked,
Nor share the sinner's way,
Or be found sitting in the scorner's seat.
2Their pleasure and passion is remaining true
To the Word of "I Am,"
Meditating each and every moment
In the revelation of light.[c]
3They will be standing firm
Like a flourishing tree planted by God's design,
Deeply rooted by the brooks of bliss;
Bearing fruit in every season of their lives.
They are never dry, never fainting,
Ever blessed, ever plentiful.
4But how different are the wicked.
All they are is dust in the wind—
Driven away to destruction![d]
5The wicked will not endure the day of judgment,
For God will not defend them.
Nothing they do will succeed or endure for long.
For they have no part with those who walk in truth,
6But how different it is for the lovers of God!
The Lord watches over them as they move forward
While the paths of the godless lead only to doom.

a Although we cannot be sure, it is possible that Ezra compiled the Psalms and wrote Psalm 1 as an "introduction" to the Psalter. Others believe it was written by David, or even Jeremiah.

b 1:1 The Hebrew text is actually "that One," and refers prophetically to the Lord Jesus Christ, our Tree of Life. Every one of us who belongs to "that One" can also walk in the light of this Psalm.

c 1:2 Or, "Torah."

d 1:4 Implied in the text.

Psalm 2

THE CORONATION OF THE KING

Act I – The Nations Speak

1 How dare the nations plan a rebellion,
Ranting and raging against the Lord Most High?
Their foolish plots are futile!
2 Look at how the power brokers of the world
Rise up to hold their summit,
Scheming and conferring together
Against God and his Anointed King, saying:
3 "Let's come together and break away from the Creator.
Once and for all let's cast off these controlling chains
Of God and his Christ!"[a]

Act II – God Speaks

4 God-Enthroned[b] merely laughs at them;
Amused at all their puny plans, mocking their madness!
5 Then with the fierceness of his fiery anger
He settles the issue,
And terrifies them to death with these words:
6 "I have poured out my King on Zion, my holy mountain.[c]
You had better listen to the One that I have chosen!"

Act III – The Son Speaks

7 "I will reveal the eternal purpose of God.
For he has decreed over me, 'You are my favored Son.
And as your Father I have crowned you as my King Eternal.
Today I have given you glory!
8 Ask me to give you the nations and I will do it,
And they shall become your legacy.

a 2:3 The word found here for *Christ* is the Hebrew word for Messiah, or Anointed One.
b 2:4 The Aramaic is *Maryah*, the Aramaic form of YHWH or Lord Jehovah.
c 2:6 For the believer today, Zion is not only a place but also a realm where Christ is enthroned. Jesus was "poured out" as an offering on our behalf.

Your domain will stretch to the ends of the earth.
9And you will rule over them with unlimited authority,
Crushing their rebellion as
An iron rod smashes jars of clay!'"

Act IV – The Holy Spirit Speaks

10Listen to me, all you rebel-kings
And all you upstart rulers of this earth!
Learn your lesson while there's still time.
11Serve and worship the awe-inspiring God.
Recognize his greatness and bow before him,
Trembling with reverence in his presence.
12Fall facedown before him
And kiss the feet of his Son
Before his anger is roused against you.
Remember that his wrath can be quickly kindled!
But many blessings are waiting for all
Who turn aside to hide themselves in him!

Psalm 3

COVERED BY THE GLORY

King David's song when he was forced
to flee from Absalom, his own son

1Lord, I have so many enemies, so many who are against me.
2Listen to how they whisper their slander against me, saying:
"Look! He's hopeless! Even God can't save him from this!"

Pause in his presence[a]

3But in the depths of my heart I truly know
That you have become my Shield;
You take me and surround me with yourself.[b]
Your glory covers me continually. You alone restore my courage;
For you lift high my head when I bow low in shame.
4I have cried out to you
And from your holy presence,
You send me a Father's help.

Pause in his presence

5So now I'll lie down and go to sleep—
And I'll awake in safety for you surround me with your glory.
6Even though dark powers prowl around me,
With their words like sharp arrows, I won't be afraid.
7I simply cry out to you:
"Rise up and help me, Lord! Come and save me!"
And you will slap them in the face,
Breaking the power of their words to harm me.

a This is the Hebrew word *Selah*, a puzzling word to translate. Most scholars believe it is a musical term for pause or rest. It is used a total of seventy-one times in the Psalms as an instruction to the music leader to pause and ponder in God's presence. An almost identical word, *Sela*, means a massive rock cliff. It is said that when *Selah* is spoken that the words are carved in stone in the throne room of the heavens.

b 3:3 Many translations render this: "You are a shield around me." The ancient Hebrew can be translated: "You, O Lord, are my Taker." The implication is that God shields us by taking us into Himself. Jesus Christ is the Taker of humanity, the One who was made flesh. He not only took our nature but He also took our sins that he might take us into glory.

8 My true Hero comes to my rescue,
For the Lord alone is my Savior.[a]
What a feast of favor and bliss he gives his people!

Pause in his presence

a 3:8 The Hebrew word used sixty times in the Psalms for deliverance is actually *Yeshuah*, a variant form of the name for *Jesus*. This is pointing us to where our salvation is found.

Psalm 4

AN EVENING PRAYER FOR HELP

For the Pure and Shining One[a]
For the end,[b] *a melody by King David*

1God, you're my righteousness, my Champion Defender,
Why aren't you answering me when I cry for help?
Whenever I was in distress you've always inspired me.
I'm being squeezed again—I need your kindness right away!
Hear my prayer and set me free!
2Listen to me, all of you who think you're great—
How long will you obscure my glory
And drag it down into shame? Will you ever stop insulting me?
How long will you set your heart on shadows,
Chasing your lies and delusions?

Pause in his presence

3May we never forget that the Lord works wonders
For every one of his chosen lovers.
And this is how I know that he will answer my every prayer.
4Tremble in awe before the Lord, and you will not sin against him.
Be still upon your bed and look deep into your heart.

Pause in his presence

5Bring your gifts just as you are and put your trust in him.
6Lord, prove them wrong when they say, "God can't help you!"
Let the light of your radiant face
Break through and shine down upon us!
7The intense pleasure you give me
Surpasses the gladness of harvest time,
Even more than when the harvesters gaze upon their ripened grain,
And when their new wine overflows.
8Now I can lay down in peace and sleep comes at once,
For no matter what happens,
I will live unafraid!

a The Hebrew word used here, usually rendered as "choirmaster" is actually taken from the root word for shining or brilliant (i.e. purity, holiness).
b As translated from the Septuagint. The Hebrew is "stringed instruments" or "smiting."

Psalm 5

SONG OF THE CLOUDED DAWN

For the Pure and Shining One
For her who receives the inheritance,[a] by King David

1Listen to my passionate prayer!
Can't you hear my groaning?
2Don't you hear how I'm crying out to you?
My King and my God, consider my every word,
For I am calling out to you.
3At each and every sunrise you will hear my voice
As I prepare my sacrifice of prayer to you.
Every morning I lay out the pieces of my life on the altar
And wait for your fire to fall upon my heart.[b]
4I know that you, God,
Are never pleased with lawlessness,
And evil ones will never be invited
As guests in your house.
5Boasters collapse, unable to survive your scrutiny,
For your hatred of evildoers is clear.
6 You will make an end of all those who lie.
How you hate their hypocrisy
And despise all who love violence!
7But I know the way back home,
And I know that you will welcome me
Into your house,
For I am covered by
Your covenant of mercy and love.
So I come to your sanctuary with deepest awe

a The Hebrew word used here is *Neliloth* or *flutes*. It can also be translated "inheritances." The early church father Augustine translated this: "For her who receives the inheritance," meaning the church of Jesus Christ. The Father told the Son in Psalm 2 to ask for his inheritance; here we see it is the church that receives what Jesus asks for. We receive our inheritance of eternal life through the cross and resurrection of the Son of God. The Septuagint reads, "For the end," also found in numerous inscriptions of the Psalms.

b 5:3 Implied in the concept of preparing the morning sacrifice. The Aramaic text states, "At dawn I shall be ready and shall appear before you."

To bow in worship and adore you.
8Lord, lead me in the pathways of your pleasure
Just like you promised me you would.
Or else my enemies will conquer me.
Smooth out your road in front of me,
Straight and level so that I will know where to walk.
9For you can't trust anything they say.
Their hearts are nothing but deep pits of destruction
Drawing people into their darkness with their speeches.
They are smooth-tongued deceivers
Who flatter with their words.
10Declare them guilty, O God!
Let their own schemes be their downfall!
Let the guilt of their sins collapse on top of them,
For they rebel against you.
11But let them all be glad,
Those who turn aside to hide themselves in you.
May they keep shouting for joy forever!
Overshadow them in your presence
As they sing and rejoice,
Then every lover of your name
Will burst forth with endless joy.
12Lord, how wonderfully you bless the righteous.
Your favor wraps around each one and
Covers them
Under your canopy of kindness and joy.

Psalm 6

A CRY FOR HEALING[a]

For the Pure and Shining One
A song for the end sung for the new day by King David

1No Lord! Don't condemn me.
Don't punish me in your fiery anger.
2Please deal gently with me;
Show me mercy for I'm sick and frail.
I'm fading away with weakness. Heal me, for I'm falling apart.
3How long until you take away this pain in my body and in my soul?
Lord, I'm trembling in fear!
4Turn back death from my door and deliver my life[b]
Because I know you love and desire to have me as your very own.
5How can I be any good to you dead?
For those who are in the graveyards sing no songs.
In the darkness of death who remembers you?
How could I bring you praise if I'm buried in a tomb?
6I'm so exhausted and worn-out with my weeping.
I endure weary, sleepless nights filled with moaning,
Soaking my pillow with my tears.
7My eyes of faith won't focus anymore, for sorrow fills my heart.
There are so many enemies who come against me!
8Go away! Leave me, all you workers of wickedness!
For the Lord has turned to listen to my thunderous cry.
9Yes! The Lord my Healer has heard all my pleading[c]
And has taken hold of my prayers and answered them all.
10Now it's my enemies who have been shamed.
Terror-stricken, they will turn back again;
Knowing the bitterness of sudden disgrace!

a Psalm 6 is a part of the daily prayer ritual of religious Jews.
b 6:4 Implied in the text.
c 6:9 Implied in the text.

Psalm 7

SONG FOR THE SLANDERED SOUL

A passionate song to the Lord to the tune of
"Breaking the Curse of Cush, the Benjamite"
by King David

1O Lord my God, I turn aside to hide my soul in you.
I trust you to save me from all those who pursue and persecute me.
2Don't leave me helpless!
Don't let my foes fall upon me like fierce lions with teeth bared.
Can't you see how they want to rip me to shreds;
Dragging me away to tear my soul to pieces?
3Lord, if I were doing evil things that would be different,
For then I would be guilty, deserving all of this.
4If I wronged someone at peace with me,
If I betrayed a friend, repaying evil for good,
Or if I have unjustly harmed my enemy,
5Then it would be right for you
To let my enemy pursue and overtake me.
In fact, let them grind me into the ground.
Let them take my life from me and drag my dignity in the dust!

Pause in his presence

6Now Lord, let your anger arise
Against the anger of my enemies.
Awaken your fury and stand up for me!
Decree that justice be done against my foes.
7Gather all the people around you.
Return to your place on high to preside over them
And once more occupy the throne of judgment.
8You are the Exalted One who judges the people,
So vindicate me publicly and restore my honor and integrity.
Before all the people declare me innocent!
9Once and for all, end the evil tactics of the wicked!
Reward and prosper the cause of the righteous,

For you are the righteous God, the Soul-Searcher,
Who looks deep into every heart
To examine the thoughts and motives.
10 God, your wrap-around presence
Is my protection, and my defense.
You bring victory to all who reach out for you.
11 Righteousness is revealed every time you judge.
Because of the strength of your forgiveness,[a]
Your anger does not break out every day,
Even though you are a righteous Judge.
12-13 Yet if the wicked do not repent,
You will not relent with your wrath;
Slaying them with your shining sword.
You are the Conqueror with an arsenal of lethal weapons
That you've prepared for them.
You have bent and strung your bow,
Making your judgment-arrows shafts of burning fire.
14-15 Look how the wicked conceive their evil schemes.
They go into labor with their lies and give birth to trouble.
They dig a pit for others to fall into,
Not knowing that they will be the very ones
That will fall into their own pit of failure.
16 For you, God, will see to it that every pit-digger
Who works to trap and harm others
Will be trapped and harmed by their own treachery.
17 But I will give all my thanks to you, Lord,
For you make everything right in the end.
I will sing my highest praise
To the God of the Highest Place![b]

a 7:11 As translated from the Septuagint.
b 7:17 Or, "to Adonai Elyon."

Psalm 8

GOD'S SPLENDOR

For the Pure and Shining One
Set to the melody of "For the Feast of Harvest"[a]
by King David

1Lord, your name is so great and powerful!
People everywhere see your splendor.
Your glorious majesty streams from the heavens,
Filling the earth with the fame of your name!
2You have built a stronghold by the songs of babies.
Strength rises up
With the chorus of singing children.
This kind of praise
Has the power to shut Satan's mouth.
Childlike worship will silence[b]
The madness of those who oppose you.
3Look at the splendor of your skies,
Your creative genius glowing in the heavens.
When I gaze at your moon and your stars
Mounted like jewels in their settings,
I know you are the Fascinating Artist
Who fashioned it all!
But when I look up and see
Such wonder and workmanship above,
I have to ask you this question:
4Compared to all this cosmic glory[c]
Why would you bother with puny, mortal man
Or be infatuated with Adam's sons?

a This inscription in the Septuagint is, "To the director over the wine vats."
b 8:2 There may be a vast difference between the glory of the heavens and the little mouths of children and babies, yet by both the majestic name of the Lord is revealed. It is amazing that perfected praises do not rise to God from the cherubim or seraphim, but from the children and babies, the weakest of humanity.
c 8:4 Implied in the text. David looked away from the darkness of earth and saw the divine order of the universe. This Psalm is meant to join the earth to the heavens, and to bring the heavenly glory into the earth, making the heavens and the earth one.

5Yet what honor you have given to man!
Created only a little lower than Elohim,[a]
Crowned like kings and queens[b]
With glory and magnificence.
6As lords of creation you have delegated to them
Mastery over all you have made.
Making everything subservient to their authority,
Placing earth itself under the feet of your image-bearers.[c]
7-8All the created order and every living thing
Of the earth, sky, and sea—
The wildest beasts and all the sea creatures,
Everything is in submission to Adam's sons.[d]
9Lord, your name is so great and powerful.
People everywhere see your majesty!
What glory streams from the heavens,
Filling the earth with the fame of your name!

a 8:5 This is the same Hebrew word used for the Creator God in Genesis 1:1.
b 8:5 The concept of kings and queens is implied in the text by the word *crowned.*
c 8:6 Implied in the text. The Septuagint translation of 8:5–7 is quoted in Hebrews 2:6–8. Today, all things are not yet under our feet. Even mosquitos still come to defeat us. But there will be a time of restoration because of Christ's redemption, when everything will rest beneath our authority. See Isaiah 11:6-9, 65:25; Matthew 19:28; & Revelation 20:4-6.
d 8:7–8 Implied in the context.

Psalm 9

TRIUMPHANT THANKS

For the Pure and Shining One
To the tune of "The Secrets of the Son"[a]
by King David

[1]Lord, I will worship you with extended hands
As my whole heart explodes with praise!
I will tell everyone everywhere about your wonderful works
And how your marvelous miracles exceed expectations!
[2]I will jump for joy and shout in triumph
As I sing your song and make music for the Most High God.
[3]For when you appear, I worship
While all of my enemies run in retreat.
They stumble and perish before your presence.
[4]For you have stood up for my cause
And vindicated me when I needed you the most.
From your righteous throne you have given me justice.
[5]With a blast of your rebuke nations are destroyed.
You obliterated their names forever and ever.
[6]The Lord thundered and our enemies have been cut off;
Vanished in everlasting ruins.
All their cities have been destroyed,
Even the memory of them has been erased.
[7]But the Lord of eternity, Our mighty God, lives and reigns forever!
He sits enthroned as King ready to render his verdicts
And judge all with righteousness.
[8]He will issue his decrees of judgment,
Deciding what is right for the entire world;
Dispensing justice to all.
[9]All who are oppressed may come to you as a
Shelter in the time of trouble, a perfect hiding place.
[10]May everyone who knows your mercy
Keep putting their trust in you,
For they can count on you for help no matter what.

a As translated by Augustine, an early church father. The Hebrew is "to the death of the Son."

O Lord, you will never, no never, neglect those who come to you.
11Listen everyone! Sing out your praises to the God
Who lives and rules within Zion!
Tell the world about all the miracles he has done!
12He tracks down killers and avenges bloodshed,
But he will never forget the ones forgotten by others,
Hearing every one of their cries for justice.
13So now, O Lord, don't forget me. Have mercy on me.
Take note of how I've been humiliated at the hands of those who hate me.
Bring me back again from the brink, from the very gates of death.
14Save me! Bring me to the spiritual gates of Ziona
So I can bring you the shout of praise you deserve.
15For the godless nations get trapped
In the very snares they set for others.
The hidden trap they set for the weak
Has snapped shut upon themselves—guilty!
16The Lord is famous for this: his justice will punish the wicked.
While they are digging a pit for others,
They are actually setting the terms for their own judgment.
They will fall into their own pit.

Consider the truth of this and pause in his presenceb

17Don't forget this: all the wicked will one day
Fall into the darkness of death's domain and remain there;
Including the nations that forget God and reject his ways.
18He will not ignore forever all the needs of the poor
For those in need shall not always be crushed.
Their hopes shall be fulfilled, for God sees it all![c]
19Lord, won't you now arise to judge and
Punish the nations who defy you?
Aren't you fed up with their rebellion?
20Make them tremble in fear before your presence.
Place a lawgiver over them,
Make them know that they are only puny, frail humans
Who must give account to you!

Pause in his presence

a 9:14 Or, "Daughter Gates of Zion."
b 9:16 The Hebrew word *Higayon* means to consider the truth of the matter.
c 9:18 Implied in the text.

Psalm 10

THE CRY OF THE OPPRESSED[a]

1Lord, you seem so far away when evil is near!
Why do you stand so far off as though you don't care?
Why have you hidden yourself when I need you the most?
2The arrogant in their elitist pride
Persecute the poor and helpless.
May you pour out upon them
The very evil they've planned against others!
3How they brag and boast of their cravings, exalting the greedy.
They congratulate themselves as they despise you.
4These arrogant ones, so smug and secure
In their delusion, the wicked boast, saying:
"God doesn't care about what we do.
There's nothing to worry about!
Our wealth will last a lifetime."
5So seemingly successful are they in their schemes,
Prosperous in all their plans and scoffing at any restraint.
Yet all this time they are unaware of his anger;
Not understanding that their day of judgment is ahead.
The Exalted God they deny will soon declare their doom!
6They boast that neither God nor men will bring them down.
They sneer at all their enemies saying in their hearts,
"We'll have success in all we do
And never have to face trouble"—
Never realizing that they are speaking this in vain.
7Their mouths spout out cursing, lies, and threats.
Only trouble and turmoil come from all their plans.
8-9Like beasts lurking in the shadows of the city
They crouch silently in ambush for the people to pass by;
Pouncing on the poor, they catch them in their snare,

a It is likely that Psalms 9 and 10 were originally one Psalm. Eight Hebrew manuscripts unite them as well as the Aramaic, Septuagint, and the Latin Vulgate. The Catholic Bible is based on the Latin Vulgate and therefore has a different numbering for the Psalms.

To murder their prey in secret!
They plunder their victims, presuming them all as inferior.[a]
10They crush the lowly as they fall beneath their brutal blows,
Watching their victims collapse in defeat!
11Then they say to themselves,
"The Lofty One is not watching while we do this.
He doesn't even care! We can get away with it!"
12Now is the time to arise, Lord! Crush them once and for all!
Don't forget the forgotten and the helpless.
13How dare the wicked think they'll escape judgment,
Believing that you would not
Call them to account for all their ways.
Don't let the wicked get away with their contempt of you!
14Lord, I know you see all that they're doing,
Noting their each and every deed.
You know the trouble and turmoil they've caused.
Now punish them thoroughly for all that they've done!
The poor and helpless ones trust in you, Lord,
For you are famous for being the Helper of the fatherless.
I know you won't let them down.
15Break the power of the wicked, and all their strong-arm tactics.
Search them out and destroy them
For the evil things they've done.
16You, Lord, are King forever and ever!
You will see to it that all the nations perish from your land.
17Lord, you know and understand all the hopes of the humble
And will hear their cries and comfort their hearts,
Helping them all!
18The orphans and the oppressed will be terrified no longer,
For you will bring them justice, And no one will trouble them.

a 10:9 Implied in the text.

Psalm 11

SONG OF THE STEADFAST

For the Pure and Shining One
by King David

1-2Lord, don't you hear
What my well-meaning friends keep saying to me:
"Run away while you can!
Fly away like a bird to hide in the mountains for safety.
For your enemies have prepared a trap for you!
They plan to destroy you with their slander and deceitful lies.
Can't you see them hiding
In their place of darkness and shadows?
They're set against you and all those who live upright lives."
But don't they know, Lord, that I have made you
My only Hiding Place.
Don't they know that I always trust in you?[a]
3 What can the righteous accomplish
When truth's pillars are destroyed and law and order collapse?
4Yet the Eternal One is never shaken—
He is still found in his temple of Holiness
Reigning as Lord and King over all.
He is closely watching everything that happens.
And with a glance, his eyes examine every heart.[b]
For his heavenly rule will prevail over all.
5He will test both the righteous and the wicked,
Exposing each heart.[c]
God's very soul detests those who love to resort to violence.
6He will rain down upon them judgment for their sins.
A scorching wind will be their portion and lot in life.
7But remember this: the Righteous Lord loves
What is right and just, and every godly one
Will come into his presence and gaze upon his face!

a 11:1–2 Implied in the text.
b 11:4 The actual Hebrew is "his eyelids." Some see the "eyelid" as the lid of the ark of covenant, which was the mercy seat.
c 11:5 Implied in the text.

Psalm 12

SONG FOR THE NEW DAY

For the Pure and Shining One
A song of smiting sung for the new day
by King David[a]

1Help, Lord! Save us! For godly ones are swiftly disappearing.
Where are the dependable, principled ones?
They're a vanishing breed!
2Everyone lies, everyone flatters, and everyone deceives.
Nothing but empty talk, smooth talk, and double-talk—
Where are the truthful?
3-4I know the Lord will not deal gently with people like that!
You will destroy every proud liar who says: "We lie all we want.
Our words are our weapons, and we won't be held accountable.
Who can stop us?"
May the Lord cut off their twisted tongues and seal their lying lips.
May they all be silenced, those that boast and brag with their
High-minded talk about doing whatever they want.
5But the Lord says, "Now I will arise! I will defend the poor,
Those who were plundered, the oppressed,
And the needy who groan for help.
I will arise to rescue and protect them!"
6For every word God speaks is sure and every promise pure.
His truth is tested, found to be flawless, and ever faithful.
It's pure as sterling silver, refined seven times in a crucible of clay.[b]
7-8Lord, you will keep us forever safe,
Out of the reach of the wicked. Even though they strut and prowl,
Tolerating and celebrating what is worthless and vile,
You will still lift up those who are yours!

a The events surrounding this Psalm could be the killing of the priests by Saul in 1 Samuel 22:17–19. Saul ordered the death of "eighty-five men who wore the linen ephod." The killing rampage continued until an entire community of priests had been slaughtered with their women and children. This great evil marked David from that day forward. The inscription found in the Septuagint is "The Eighth Psalm of David."

b 12:6 The clay furnace is the heart of man. We are the earthen vessel inside which God has placed his flawless words. His words test us, they try us, and they refine us, seven times over, until purified and assimilated into our spirits. The fire of testing purifies us as vessels to carry the Word within our hearts.

Psalm 13

PRAYER TURNS DEPRESSION INTO DELIGHT[a]

For the Pure and Shining One
by King David

1I'm hurting, Lord—will you forget me forever?[b]
How much longer, Lord?
Will you look the other way when I'm in need?[c]
2How much longer must I cling to this constant grief?
I've endured this shaking of my soul.
So, how much longer
Will my enemy have the upper hand?
It's been long enough!
3Take a good look at me, God, and answer me!
Breathe your life into my spirit.
Bring light to my eyes in this pitch-black darkness
Or I will sleep the sleep of death.
4Don't let my enemy proclaim,
"I've prevailed over him."
For all my adversaries will celebrate when I fall.
5Lord, I have always trusted in your kindness,
So answer me, for I know you won't fail me now.[d]
I will yet celebrate with passion and joy
When your salvation[e] lifts me up.
6I will sing my song of joy to you, the Most High,
For in all of this you have strengthened my soul.
My enemies say that I have no Savior,
But I know that I have one in you!

a Some believe David composed this shortly after being anointed to be the King of Israel. David knew greatness was his destiny, but he struggled with the persecution and challenges that came before his exaltation. In the wilderness David trusts and prays his way out.

b 13:1 This is the Psalm that describes the journey from self to God, from despair to delight, from feeling abandoned to feeling affirmed. It begins with pain and ends with praise. Moaning gives way to music. We each can take comfort in what David experienced.

c 13:1 David feels as though God is hiding his face from his cries. David is left alone to wrestle with his doubts, feeling as though his patience can hold on no longer. Have you ever been there?

d 13:5 Implied in the text.

e 13:5 The term for *salvation* is *yeshu'sh*, which is nearly identical to *Jesus, our Salvation*. Our Savior plans blessings and hope for each of us as we trust in him.

Psalm 14

GOD LOOKS DOWN FROM HEAVEN[a]

For the Pure and Shining One
by King David

1Only the withering soul would say to himself,[b]
"There is no God."
Anyone who thinks like this is corrupt and callous,
Depraved and detestable, devoid of what is good.
2The Lord looks down in love,
Bending over heaven's balcony,
Looking over all of Adam's sons and daughters.
He's looking to see if there is anyone
Who is wise and has insight;
Any who are searching for God and wanting to please him.
3But no, everyone has wandered astray,
Walking stubbornly toward evil.
Not one is good; he can't even find one.
4Look how they live in luxury while exploiting my people!
Won't these workers of wickedness ever learn?
They don't ever even think of praying to God.
5But just look at them now, in panic; trembling with terror.
For the Lord is on the side of the generation of loyal lovers.
6The Lord is always the safest place for the poor
When the workers of wickedness oppress them.
7How I wish their time of rescue were already here,
And that God would appear;
Arising from the midst of his Zion-people
To save and restore his very own.
Then what gladness and joy will break forth
When the Lord rescues Israel!

a With few differences, Psalm 14 and Psalm 53 are nearly identical. Psalm 14 is practical; Psalm 53 is prophetic. Psalm 14 deals with the past, Psalm 53 with the future.

b 14:1 The word for *fool* comes from a Hebrew word meaning withering. If we make no room for God, we have a withered heart; and our moral sense of righteousness is put to sleep, and the noble aspirations of the heart shrivel up and die.

Psalm 15

LIVING IN THE SHINING PLACE[a]

A poetic song by King David

1Lord, who dares to dwell with you?
Who presumes the privilege
Of being close to you;
Living next to you in your shining place of glory?[b]
Who are those who daily dwell
In the life of the Holy Spirit?[c]
2They are passionate and wholehearted,
Always sincere and always speaking the truth—
For their hearts are trustworthy.
3They refuse to slander[d] or insult others,
They'll never listen to gossip or rumors,
Nor would they ever harm another with their words.
4They will speak out passionately against evil, and evil workers;
While commending the faithful ones
Who follow after the truth.
They make firm commitments and follow through, even at great cost.
5They never crush others with exploitation or abuse
And they would never be bought with a bribe against the innocent.
They're the ones who will enter into the life of the Spirit.
Never shaken, they will stand firm forever.

a Perhaps David's prophetic minstrels sang this song of instruction as they laid the ark to rest in David's tent. It is a song that reveals who will dwell in God's holy presence and who will live with him in heaven's glory. It actually is a description of Zion's perfect Man, *Christ Jesus*, and all those who are transformed into his image (Romans 8:29).

b 15:1 The Hebrew word for *sanctuary* is taken from a root word for "shining place."

c 15:1 This Psalm gives us David's Sermon on the Mount. If we will dwell in the Holy Place, there must first be a holy place in our spirit where God dwells. God's guests must submit to the holiness that lives there. There is etiquette for God's house revealed in this Psalm.

d 15:3 The Hebrew word for slander, *ragal*, means to spy on someone and look for evil to use against them.

Psalm 16

THE GOLDEN SECRET

A precious song, engraved in gold, by King David[a]

1Keep me safe, O mighty God,
I run for dear life to you, my Safe Place.
2So I say to the Lord God,
You are my Maker, my Mediator, and my Master.
You don't need my "goodness,"
For I have none apart from you.[b]
3And he said to me,[c] "My holy lovers are wonderful,
My majestic ones, my glorious ones,
Fulfilling all my desires."
4Yet, there are those who yield to their weakness,[d]
And they will have troubles and sorrows unending.
I never gather with such ones,[e]
Nor give them honor in any way.
5Lord, I have chosen you alone as my inheritance.
You are my prize, my pleasure, and my portion.
I leave my destiny and its timing in your hands.[f]
6Your pleasant path leads me to pleasant places.
I'm overwhelmed by the privileges
That come with following you,
For you have given me the best!
7The way you counsel and correct me
Makes me praise you more;
For your whispers in the night give me wisdom,

a The Hebrew word used in the inscription is *michtam*. There are many variations of translation for this word. Here are the major ones: *golden, graven, a permanent writing, precious, hidden, or jewel.* The Septuagint renders this: "a sculptured writing of gold"; while other translations call it a "golden poem." Perhaps the most accepted translation of *michtam* is "engraved in gold." This speaks of the divine nature engraved into our hearts by the Word. A new humanity is now stamped with God-life, engraved in his golden glory.

b 16:2 The Aramaic text states, "My goodness is found in your presence."

c 16:3 Implied in the text.

d 16:4 As translated from the Septuagint.

e 16:4 As translated from the Septuagint.

f 16:5 Implied in the text. The Aramaic reads, "You are restoring my inheritance to me."

Showing me what to do next.
8Because you are close to me and always available,
My confidence will never be shaken,
For I experience your wrap-around presence every moment.
9My heart and soul explode with joy—full of glory!
Even my body will rest confident and secure.
10For you will not abandon me to the realm of death
Nor will you allow your Holy One to experience corruption.
11For you bring me a continual revelation of resurrection life,[a]
The path to the bliss
That brings me face-to-face with you.[b]

a 16:11 Implied in the context.
b 16:11 There is no Hebrew word for *presence*. When the Psalmist wanted to speak of God's presence, he used the Hebrew word for face.

Psalm 17

A CRY FOR JUSTICE

A priestly prayer by King David

1Listen to me, Lord,
Hear the passionate prayer of this honest man.
It's my piercing cry for justice!
My cause is just and my need is real.
I've done what's right and my lips speak truth.
2Lord, I always live my life before your face,
So examine and exonerate me.
Vindicate me and show the world I'm innocent.
3For in a visitation of the night
You inspected my heart and refined my soul in fire
Until nothing vile was found in me.
I've wanted my words and my ways to always agree.
4Following your Word has kept me from wrong.
Your ways have molded my footsteps, keeping me
From going down the forbidden paths of the destroyer.
5My steps follow in the tracks of your chariot wheels,
Always staying in their path,
Never straying from your way.
6You will answer me, God; I know you always will,
Like you always do as you listen with love to my every prayer.
7 Magnify the marvels of your mercy to all who seek you.[a]
Make your Pure One wonderful to me,[b]
Like you do for all those who turn aside
To hide themselves in you.
8Protect me from harm, keep an eye on me,
Like you would a child[c]
Reflected in the twinkling of your eye.

a 17:7 As translated from the Septuagint.
b 17:7 As translated from the Aramaic.
c 17:8 Or, "daughter."

Yes, hide me within the shelter of your embrace,
Under the wings of your covering-cherubim.[a]
9Protect me there from all my foes.
For there are many who surround my soul
To completely destroy me.
10They are pitiless, heartless—hard as nails,
Swollen with pride and filled with arrogance!
11See how they close in on me, waiting for the chance
To throw me to the ground.[b]
12They're like lions eager to tear me apart;
Like young and fearless lions lurking in secret,
So ferocious and cruel—ready to rip me to shreds.
13Arise, God, and confront them!
Challenge them with your might![c]
Free me from their clutches and rescue me from their rage.
14Throw them down to the ground,
These who live for only this life on earth.
Thrust them out of their prosperity
And into their portion in eternity,
Leaving their wealth and wickedness behind!
15As for me, because I am innocent I will see[d] your face,
Until I see you for who you really are.
Then I will awaken with your form
And be fully satisfied,[e] fulfilled in the revelation
Of your glory in me!

a 17:8 This becomes a reference to the mercy seat, where sacred blood was sprinkled in the Holy of Holies. There the golden cherubim overshadowed all who entered the divine chamber (Exodus 25:18–20).
b 17:11 This is what they did to Jesus. They threw him to the ground and nailed him to the cross.
c 17:13 The word used here is *sword*. An alternative translation would be, "Rescue my soul from the wicked one, who is your sword." The wicked are sometimes God's tools to execute his judgments (Isaiah 10:5; Jeremiah 51:20).
d 17:15 The Hebrew word for gaze, *chaza*, means "to see a vision."
e 17:15 The Aramaic can be translated, "I will be satisfied when your faith is awakened."

Psalm 18

I LOVE YOU, LORD

Praises sung to the Pure and Shining One
by King David, his servant,[a] *composed when the Lord rescued David*
from all his many enemies, including from the brutality of Saul[b]

1Lord, I passionately love you! I want to embrace you,[c]
For now you've become my Power!
2You're as real to me as Bedrock beneath my feet,
Like a Castle on a cliff, my forever firm Fortress,
My Mountain of hiding, my Pathway of escape,
My Tower of rescue where none can reach me,
My secret Strength and Shield around me,
You are Salvation's Ray of Brightness
Shining on the hillside,[d]
Always the Champion of my cause.
3So all I need to do is to call on to you
Singing to you, the praiseworthy God.
And when I do, I'm safe and sound in you.
4-5For when the spirit of death wrapped chains around me [e]
And terrifying torrents of destruction overwhelmed me,
Taking me to death's door, to doom's domain;
6I cried out to you in my distress, the delivering God,
And from your temple-throne
You heard my troubled cry.
My sobs came right into your heart
And you turned your face to rescue me.[f]
7The earth itself shivered and shook.

a This magnificent poem is so important to the Holy Spirit that it appears twice in the Bible. You will find it again in 2 Samuel 22.
b Or, "the paw of Saul." He was like a beast that chased David until his death.
c 18:1 The Hebrew word used here for "love" is not the usual word to describe love. It is a fervent and passionate word that carries the thought of embrace and touch. It could actually be translated, "Lord, I want to hug you!" Haven't you ever felt like that?
d 18:2 The Hebrew word for "horn" (i.e., horn of my salvation) comes from a root word meaning ray of brightness or hillside. The translator has chosen to include both concepts in the translation.
e 18:4-5 Or, "When the flood of Belial made me afraid."
f 18:6 This scene is a poetic portrayal not only of how God answered David's prayer, but also a picture of the sufferings of a greater Son of David, Jesus, who hung on the cross with cries of agony. God heard him and shook the planet as thick clouds covered the sun.

It reeled and rocked before him.
As the mountains melted, they melted away!
For his anger was kindled, burning on my behalf.
8Fierce flames leapt from his mouth, erupting with blazing,
Burning coals as smoke and fire encircled him.
9-10He stretched heaven's curtain open
And came to my defense.
Swiftly he rode to earth as the the stormy sky was lowered.
He rode a chariot of thunderclouds amidst thick darkness.
A cherub, his steed, as he swooped down,
Soaring on the wings of spirit-wind.
11Wrapped and hidden in the thick-cloud darkness,
His thunder-tabernacle surrounding him.
He hid himself in mystery-darkness;
The dense rain clouds were his garments.
12Suddenly the brilliance of his presence breaks through
With lightning bolts, and with a mighty storm from heaven.
Like a tempest dropping coals of fire.
13The Lord thunders, the great God above every god
Speaks with his thunder-voice from the skies.
What fearsome hailstones and flashes of fire before him!
14He releases his lightning-arrows, and routed my foes.
See how they run and scatter in fear!
15Then with his mighty roar
He lays bare the foundations of the earth,
Uncovering the secret source of the sea.
Look! The hidden depths of land and sea are now exposed
By the hurricane-blast of his hot-breath.
16He then reached down from heaven,
All the way from the sky to the sea.
He reached down into my darkness to rescue me!
He took me out of my calamity and chaos
And drew me to himself,
Taken from the depths of my despair!
17Even though I was helpless in the hands
Of my hateful, strong enemy,[a]

a 18:17 Death is our strong enemy. Only through Christ are we delivered from its grip.

You were good to deliver me.
18When I was at my weakest, my enemies attacked—
But the Lord held on to me.
19His love broke open the way
And he brought me into a beautiful broad place.[a]
He rescued me—because his delight is in me![b]
20He rewarded me for doing what's right and staying pure.
21I will follow his commands and never stop.
I'll not sin by ceasing to follow him no matter what.
22For I've kept my eyes focused on his righteous words
And I've obeyed everything that he's told me to do.
23I've done my best to be blameless, and to follow all his ways,
Keeping my heart pure.
24I've kept my integrity by surrendering to him.
And so the Lord has rewarded me with his blessing.
This is the treasure I discovered
When I kept my heart clean before his eyes.
25Lord, it is clear to me now that how we live
Will dictate how you deal with us.[c]
Good people will taste your goodness, Lord.
And those who are loyal to you,
You love to prove that you are loyal and true.
26And for those who are purified, they find you always pure.
But you'll outwit the crooked and cunning with your craftiness.
27To the humble you bring heaven's deliverance.
But the proud and haughty you disregard.
28God, all at once, you turned on a floodlight for me!
You are the revelation light in my darkness,
And in your brightness I can see the path ahead.
29With you as my strength I can crush an enemy horde
Advancing through every stronghold
That stands in front of me.
30What a God you are! Your path for me has been perfect!

a 18:19 This could be the throne room of heaven.
b 18:19 Here in verses 16–19 you can see the glorious resurrection of Christ as the Father reached down and kissed the Son with life and love. Read it again and think of Christ in the tomb being raised by the Father.
c 18:25 This is a summary of the passage, implied in the text.

All your promises have proven true.
What a secure shelter for all those
Who turn to hide themselves in you!
You are the wrap-around God giving grace to me.[a]
31Could there be any other god like you?
You are the only God to be worshipped,
For there is not a more secure foundation
To build my life upon than you.
32You have wrapped me in power,
And now you've shared with me your perfection.
33Through you I ascend to the highest peaks of your glory
To stand in the heavenly places, strong and secure in you.
34You've trained me with the weapons of warfare-worship;
Now I'll descend down into battle with power,
To chase and conquer my foes.
35You empower me for victory with
Your wrap-around presence.
Your power within makes me strong to subdue,
And by stooping down in gentleness
You strengthened me, and made me great!
36You've set me free from captivity
And now I'm standing complete, ready to fight some more!
37I caught up with my enemies and conquered them,
And didn't turn back until the war was won!
38I pinned them to the ground and broke them to pieces.
I finished them once and for all; they're as good as dead.
39You've placed your armor upon me
And defeated my enemies, making them bow low at my feet.
40You've made them all turn tail and run,
For through you I've destroyed them all!
Forever silenced they'll never taunt me again.
41They shouted for help but not one dares to rescue them.
They shouted to God but he refused to answer them.
42So I pulverized them to powder and cast them to the wind.
I swept them away like dirt on the floor.

a 18:30 The Hebrew word used here for *shield* means to wrap around in protection. God himself is our shield of grace.

43You gave me victory on every side,
For look how the nations come to serve me.
Even those I've never heard of come and bow at my feet.
44As soon as they heard of me they submitted to me.
Even the rebel foreigners obey my every word.
45Their rebellion fades away as they come near;
Trembling in their strongholds
They come crawling out of their hideouts,
Cringing in fear before me, their courage is gone.
46The Almighty is alive and conquers all!
Praise is lifted high to the unshakable God!
Towering over all, my Savior-God is worthy to be praised!
47Look how he pays back harm to all who harm me,
Subduing all the people who come against me.
48He rescues me from my enemies;
He lifts me up high and keeps me out of reach,
Far from the grasp of my violent foe.
49This is why I thank God with high praises!
I will sing my song to the Highest God,
So all among the nations will hear me.
50You have appointed me king and rescued me
Time and time again with your magnificent miracles.
You've been merciful and kind to me, your anointed one.
This favor will be forever seen upon
Your loving servant, David,
And to all my true seed, every heir of this promise![a]

a 18:50 Implied in the text.

Psalm 19

GOD'S WITNESSES

For the Pure and Shining One
A poem of praise by King David, his loving servant

[God's Story in the Skies]

1God's splendor is a tale that is told;
His testament is written in the stars.[a]
Space itself speaks his story every day
Through the marvels of the heavens.
His truth is on tour in the starry-vault of the sky,
Showing his skill in creation's craftsmanship.
2Each day gushes out its message[b] to the next,
Night with night whispering its knowledge to all.
3Without a sound, without a word,
Without a voice being heard,
4Yet all the world can see its story,
Everywhere its gospel[c]
Is clearly read so all may know.
5What a heavenly home God has set for the sun,
Shining in the superdome of the sky!
See how he leaves his celestial chamber each morning,
Radiant as a bridegroom ready for his wedding,
Like a day-breaking champion eager to run his course.
6He rises on one horizon, completing his circuit on the other;
Warming lives and lands with his heat.

[God's Story in the Scriptures]

7God's Word is perfect in every way,
How it revives our souls!
His laws lead us to truth,

a 19:1 Or, "The heavens are continually rehearsing the glory of God."
b 19:2 Or, "speaks its prophecy."
c 19:4 Literal translation from the Aramaic. There are many who believe that constellations (Heb. *mazzarot*) of the sky bring us the revelation of the gospel of Jesus Christ. A message is being given without words, sound, or a voice. See Job 38:31–33.

And his ways change the simple into wise.
8His teachings make us joyful and radiate his light;
His precepts are so pure!
His commands, how they challenge us
To keep close to his heart!
The revelation-light of his Word makes my spirit shine radiant.
9Living my life in the holy fear of God keeps me faithful,
And to follow him keeps me full of life.
Nothing he says ever needs to be changed.
10The rarest treasures of life are found in his truth.
That's why I prize God's Word like others prize the finest gold.
Nothing brings the soul such sweetness
As seeking his living words.
11For they warn us, his servants,
And keep us from following the wicked way,
Giving a lifetime guarantee:
Great success to every obedient soul!
12Without this revelation light[a]
How would I ever detect
The waywardness of my heart?[b]
Lord, forgive my hidden flaws whenever you find them.
13Keep cleansing me, God,
And keep me from my secret, selfish sins;
May they never rule over me!
For only then will I be free from fault
And remain innocent of rebellion.
14So may the words of my mouth,
My meditation-thoughts,
And every movement of my heart
Be always pure and pleasing,
Acceptable before your eyes,
My only Redeemer, my Protector-God.[c]

a 19:12 Implied in the text.
b 19:12 The word *waywardness* is taken from the Hebrew word for errors.
c 19:14 Implied in the text.

Psalm 20

A SONG OF TRUST

For the Pure and Shining One
For the end times by King David[a]

1In your day of danger may the Lord answer and deliver you!
May the name of the God of Grace set you safely on high! [b]
2May supernatural help be sent from his sanctuary!
May he support you from Zion's fortress!
3May he remember every gift you have given him,
And celebrate every sacrifice of love you have shown him.

Pause in his presence

4May God give you every desire of your heart
And carry out your every plan as you go to battle. [c]
5When you succeed we will celebrate and shout for joy.
Flags will fly when victory is yours!
Yes, God will answer your prayers and we will praise him!
6I know God gives me all that I ask for
And brings victory to his anointed king.
My deliverance cry will be heard in his holy heaven.
Through his mighty hand
Miracles will manifest through his saving strength.
7Some find their strength in their weapons and wisdom,
But my miracle deliverance can never be won by men.
Our boast is in the Lord our God who
Makes us strong and gives us victory!
8Our enemies will not prevail; they will only collapse and
Perish in defeat while we will rise up, full of courage.
9Give victory to our king, O God!
The day we call on you, give us your answer!

a The inscription for Psalm 20–22 is "For the End Times," as translated from the Septuagint.
b 20:1 The name used for *God* here is "The God of Jacob." Jacob was one transformed by God's grace, changed from a schemer who took from others, into Israel, God's prince.
c 20:4 Implied in the context.

Psalm 21

THROUGH YOUR STRENGTH

For the end time, to the Pure and Shining One
King David's poem of praise

1Lord, because of your strength the king is strong.
Look how he rejoices in you![a]
He bursts out with a joyful song because of your victory!
2For you have given him his heart's desire,
Anything and everything he asks for.
You haven't withheld a thing from your betrothed one.

Pause in his presence

3Rich blessings overflow with every encounter with you,
And you placed a royal crown of gold upon his head.
4He wanted resurrection—you have given it to him and more!
The days of his blessing stretch on
One after another, forever!
5You have honored him and made him famous.
Glory garments are upon him,
And you surround him with splendor and majesty.
6Your victory heaps blessing after blessing upon him.
What joy and bliss he tastes, rejoicing before your face!
7For the king trusts endlessly in you,
And he will never stumble, never fall.
Your forever-love never fails and holds him firm.
8Your almighty hands have captured your foes.
You uncovered all who hate you and you seized them.
9-10When you appear before them,
Unveiling the radiance of your face,[b]
They will be consumed by the fierce fire of your presence.
Flames will swallow them up.
They and their descendants will be destroyed by an unrelenting fire.

a 21:1 Think of this song as a praise song to Jesus, our true King.
b 21:9–10 Implied in the text.

11 We will watch them fail, for these are ones
Who plan their evil schemes against the Lord.
12 They will turn and run at the sight
Of your judgment-arrow aimed straight at their hearts.
13 Rise up and put your might on display!
By your strength we will sing and praise your glorious power!

Psalm 22

A PROPHETIC PORTRAIT OF THE CROSS[a]

For the Pure and Shining One
King David's song of anguish,
to the tune of "The Deer Giving Birth at the Day-Dawning"[b]

1God, my God!
Why would you abandon me now?[c]
2Why do you remain distant,
Refusing to answer[d] my tearful cries in the day
And my desperate cries for your help in the night?
I can't stop sobbing.
Where are you, my God?
3Yet, I know that you are most holy; it's indisputable.
You are God-Enthroned, surrounded with songs,
Living among the shouts of praise of your princely people.
4Our fathers' faith was in you—
Through the generations they trusted and believed in you
And you came through.
5Every time they cried out to you in their despair,
You were faithful to deliver them;
You didn't disappoint them.
6But look at me now, I am like a woeful worm,
Crushed, and I'm bleeding crimson.[e]
I don't even look like a man anymore.
I've been abused, despised, and scorned by everyone!

a There were thirty-three distinct prophecies from this Psalm that were fulfilled when Jesus was on the cross.

b This could be an amazing picture of Christ giving birth at the cross to a generation of his seed. They are like children of God born in the dawning of that resurrection morning.

c 22:1 When Jesus quoted these words dying on the cross, he was identifying himself as the One David wrote about in this Psalm. It is a breathtaking portrayal of what Jesus endured through his suffering for us. The Psalm ends with another quotation of Jesus on the cross: "It is finished!"

d 22:2 David uses poetic nuance here, for the word *answer* (*'anah*) is also a Hebrew homonym for affliction.

e 22:6 The Hebrew word for *worm is tola*, which is also the word for *crimson* or *scarlet*. *Tola* was a certain worm in the Middle East that, when crushed, bled a crimson color so strong it was used as a dye for garments. Jesus was not saying he is a despised worm, but that he will bleed as he is crushed for our sins.

7Mocked by their jeers, despised with their sneers,
Spitting their insults, as all the people poke fun at me.
8Saying, "Is this the one who trusted in God?
Is this the one who claims God is pleased with him?
Now let's see if your God will come to your rescue!
We'll just see how much he delights in you!"
9Lord, you delivered me safely from my mother's womb.
You are the One who cared for me ever since I was a baby.
10Since the day I was born I've been placed in your custody.
You've cradled me throughout my days.
I've trusted in you and you've always been my God.
11So don't leave me now, stay close to me!
For trouble is all around me
And there's no one else to help me.
12I'm surrounded by many violent foes;
Mighty forces of evil are swirling around me
That want to break me to bits and destroy me.[a]
13Curses pour from their mouths!
They're like ravenous, roaring lions tearing their prey.
14Now I'm completely exhausted, I'm spent.
Every joint of my body has been pulled apart.
My courage has vanished and
My inward parts have melted away.
15I'm so thirsty and parched—dry as a bone.
My tongue sticks to the roof of my mouth.
And now you've left me in the dust for dead.
16They have pierced my hands and my feet.
Like a pack of wild dogs they tear at me,
Swirling around me with their hatred.
They gather around me like lions
To pin[b] my hands and feet.
17All my bones stick out.
Look at how they all gloat over me and stare!

a 22:12 Many translations have here "strong bulls of Bashan." The translator sees here the forces of darkness, evil spirits, that surrounded Jesus, taunting and tormenting him while on the cross. The root word for *bull* means to break or destroy. The word *Bashan*, although known as a fertile land northeast of the Sea of Galilee, is also a word for serpent. These represent the many demonic spirits who came against the Son of God as he was being crucified.

b 22:16 Or, "to maul" or "to pierce."

18With a toss of the dice they divide
My clothes among themselves,
Gambling for my garments!
19Lord, my God, please don't stay far away.
For you are my only might and strength;
Won't you come quickly to my rescue?
20Give me back my life. Save me from this violent death;
Save my precious one and only[a]
From the power of these demon.![b]
21Save me from all the power of the enemy;
From this roaring lion raging against me
And the power of his dark horde.
22I will praise your name before all my brothers;
As my people gather I will praise you in their midst.[c]
23Lovers of Yahweh, praise him!
Let all the true seed of Jacob glorify him with your praises.
Stand in awe of him,
All you princely people, the offspring of Israel!
24For he has not despised my cries of deep despair.
He's my First Responder to my sufferings,
And he didn't look the other way when I was in pain.
He was there all the time,
Listening to the song of the afflicted.
25You're reason for my praise; it comes from you and goes to you.
I will keep my promise to praise you before all who fear you
Among the congregation of your people.
26I will invite the poor and broken
And they will come and eat until satisfied.
Bring Yahweh praise and you will find him.
Your hearts will overflow with outrageous joy![d]
27From the four corners of the earth,

a 22:20 Or, "unique," or, "darling." We are that *one and only* child and "unique darling" here in this Psalm. See also Song of Songs 6:9. On the cross, Jesus—like a deer giving birth at the dawning light (see inscription of Psalm 22)—cared less that his body was being torn apart, and more for our protection and salvation. He prayed for us as he faced the death of the cross.

b 22:20 The Hebrew text uses the word *dogs*, which implies evil spirits who were bent on destroying Jesus on the cross. The Hebrew word for *dog* is taken from a root word meaning to attack.

c 22:22 Between verse 21 and verse 22 the glorious resurrection of Jesus takes place. The music is elevated to a higher key as victory is sounded forth. "My people gather" is a reference to the church that was birthed through his resurrection glory. (See also verse 25.)

d 22:26 Implied in the text.

The peoples of the world
Will remember and return to the Lord.
Every nation will come and worship him.
28For the Lord is King of all,
Who takes charge of all the nations.
29There they are! They're worshipping!
The wealthy of this world
Will feast in fellowship with him
Right alongside the humble of heart,
Bowing down to the dust, forsaking their own souls.
They will all come and worship this worthy King!
30His spiritual seed shall serve him.
Future generations will hear from us
About the wonders of the Sovereign Lord.
31His generation yet to be born will glorify him.
And they will all declare: "It is finished!"

Psalm 23

THE GOOD SHEPHERD

David's poetic praise to God[a]

1The Lord is my Fierce Protector and my Pastor.[b]
I always have more than enough.
2He offers a resting place for me
In his luxurious love.
His tracks take me to an oasis of peace,
The quiet brook of bliss.
3That's where he restores and revives my life.
He opens before me pathways to God's pleasure,
And leads me along in his footsteps of righteousness,
So that I can bring honor to his name.
4Lord, even when your path takes me through
The valley of deepest darkness
Fear will never conquer me, for you already have!
You remain close to me and lead me through it all the way.
Your authority is my strength and my peace.[c]
The comfort of your love takes away my fear.
I'll never be lonely, for you are near.[d]
5You become my delicious feast
Even when my enemies dare to fight.
You anoint me with the fragrance of your Holy Spirit;[e]
You give me all I can drink of you until my heart overflows.
6So why would I fear the future?
For I'm being pursued only by

a Most scholars conclude that Psalm 23 was written by David when he was a young shepherd serving his father, Jesse, while he was keeping watch over sheep near Bethlehem. He was most likely sixteen or seventeen years old. The other Psalm that he wrote when but a young lad was Psalm 19. Those are two good Psalms to memorize and meditate upon if you want to have the heart of the giant-killer.

b 23:1 The word most commonly used here is *shepherd.* In the days when David wrote this, a shepherd was as much a warrior as a gentle caregiver for sheep. Living in the wilderness with wild beasts, shepherds were both brave and strong.

c 23:4 Or, "Your rod and your staff, they comfort me."

d 23:4 Implied in the text.

e 23:5 The word *oil* becomes a symbol of the Holy Spirit.

Your goodness and unfailing love.
Then afterwards—when my life is through,
I'll return to your glorious presence
To be forever with you!

Psalm 24

THE GLORIOUS KING

David's poetic praise to God[a]

1God claims the world as his!
Everything and everyone belongs to him!
2He's the One who pushed back oceans
To let the dry ground appear;
Planting firm foundations for the earth.
3Who, then, ascends into the presence of the Lord?
And who has the privilege of entering
Into God's holy place?
4Those who are clean—whose works and ways are pure;
Whose hearts are true and sealed by the truth;
Those who never deceive, whose words are sure.
5They will receive the Lord's blessing,
And righteousness given by the Savior-God.
6They will stand before God.
For they seek the pleasure of God's face,[b] the God of Jacob.

Pause in his presence

7So wake up, you living gateways!
Lift up your heads, you ageless doors of destiny!
Welcome the King of Glory,
For he is about to come through you.
8You ask, "Who is this Glory-King?"
The Lord, armed and ready for battle,
The Mighty One, invincible in every way!
9So wake up, you living gateways, and rejoice![c]
Fling wide, you ageless doors of destiny!
Here he comes; the King of Glory is ready to come in.

a The Septuagint adds "for the Sabbath."
b 24:6 The Hebrew is plural ("faces").
c 24:9 The Hebrew text says, "lift up your heads," which is a figure of speech for rejoicing. We are the living gateways who rejoice as the Lord draws near to us from his temple.

10You ask, "Who is this King of Glory?"
He's the Lord of Victory, armed and ready for battle,
The Mighty One, the invincible Commander of heaven's hosts!
Yes, he is the King of Glory!

Pause in his presence

Psalm 25

DON'T FAIL ME, GOD![a]

King David's poetic praise to God

1Forever I will lift up my soul into your presence, Lord.
2Be there for me, God, for I keep trusting in you.
Don't allow my foes to gloat over me or
The shame of defeat to overtake me.
3For how could anyone be disgraced
When they've entwined their hearts with you?
But they will all be defeated and ashamed
When they harm the innocent.
4Lord, direct me throughout my journey,
So I can experience your plans for my life.
Reveal the life-paths that are pleasing to you.
5Escort me along the way, take me by the hand and teach me,
For you are the God of my increasing salvation;
I have wrapped my heart into yours![b]
6-7Forgive my failures as a young man,
And overlook the sins of my immaturity.
Give me grace, Lord! Always look at me
Through your eyes of love—
Your forgiving eyes of mercy and compassion.
When you think of me, see me as one you love and care for.
How good you are to me!
8When someone turns to you
They discover how easy you are to please—
So faithful and true!
Joyfully you teach them the proper path,
Even when they go astray.

a Psalms 25–39 are fifteen poetic songs of bringing pure worship before God. Psalms 25–29 speak of our confidence to worship God. Psalms 30–34 point us to receiving life eternal from our Hero-God. And the last five, Psalms 35–39, bring us to the importance of personal purity and holiness before God as we worship him in truth.

b 25:5 The Hebrew word most commonly translated as *wait* (wait upon the Lord) is *qavah,* which also means to tie together by twisting, or entwine, or wrap tightly. This is a beautiful concept of waiting upon God, not as something passive, but entwining our hearts with him and his purposes.

9Keep showing the humble your path,
And lead them into the best decision—
Bring revelation light that trains them in the truth.
10May they obey you, and follow you
In the pleasant paths of love and faithfulness!
For your love surrounds them
As your truth takes them forward.
11For the honor of your name, Lord,
Never count my sins and forgive them all—
Lift their burden off of my life![a]
12But still one question remains:
How do I live in the holy fear of God?
Show me the right path to take.
13Then prosperity and favor will be my portion,
And my descendants will inherit all that is good.
14There's a private place reserved for the lovers of God,
Where they sit near him and receive
The revelation-secrets of his promises.[b]
15Rescue me, Lord,
For you're my only Hero.
16Sorrows fill my heart as I feel helpless, mistreated—
I'm all alone, and in misery!
Come closer to me now, Lord,
For I need your mercy.
17Turn to me, for my problems
Seem to be going from bad to worse.
Only you can free me from all these troubles!
18Until you lift this burden,
The burden of all my sins,
My troubles and trials will be more than I can handle.
Can't you feel my pain?
19Vicious enemies hate me.
There are so many, Lord, can't you see?

a 25:11 The Hebrew word used here for *forgive* or *pardon* is a rare word only used twice in the Old Testament and comes from a root word meaning to lift off a burden.
b 25:14 Or, "covenant." The Hebrew word for *secret* is actually the word for *couch*. This is the place intimate friends would sit together to talk, to share secrets.

[20]Will you protect me from their power against me?
Let it never be said that I trusted you
And you didn't come to my rescue.
[21]Your perfection and faithfulness are my bodyguards,
For you are my hope and I trust in you as my only protection.
[22]Zealously, God, we ask you
To come save Israel from all her troubles,
For you provide the ransom price for your people![a]

a Psalm 25 is an acrostic Psalm—that is, in the Hebrew text every verse begins with a progressive letter of the alphabet. It is considered a poetic device of Hebrew literature. Go back through the Psalm and notice how almost every verse begins with the next letter of our English alphabet. See if you can find them. (*X* was not included.)

Psalm 26

DECLARE ME INNOCENT

King David's poetic praise to God

[1]You be my Judge and declare me innocent!
Clear my name, for I have tried my best to keep your laws
And to trust you without wavering.
[2]Lord, you can scrutinize me.
Refine my heart and probe my every thought.
Put me to the test and you'll find it's true.
[3]I will never lose sight of your love for me.
Your faithfulness has steadied my steps.
[4]I won't keep company with tricky, two-faced men,
Nor will I go the way of those
Who defraud with hidden motives.
[5]I despise the sinner's hangouts,
Refusing to even enter them.
You won't find me walking among the wicked.
[6-7]When I come before you, I'll come clean,
Approaching your altar with songs of thanksgiving;
Singing the songs of your mighty miracles.
[8]Lord, I love your home, this place of dazzling glory,
Bathed in the splendor and light of your presence!
[9]Don't treat me as one of these scheming sinners
Who plot violence against the innocent.
[10]Look how they devise their wicked plans;
Holding the innocent hostage for ransom.
[11]I'm not like them, Lord—not at all.
Save me, redeem me with your mercy,
For I have chosen to walk only in what is right.
[12]I will proclaim it publicly in every congregation,
And because of you, Lord,
I will take my stand on righteousness alone!

Psalm 27

FEARLESS FAITH

David's poetic praise to God before he was anointed king[a]

1The Lord is my Revelation Light
To guide me along the way;[b]
He's the Source of my salvation
To defend me every day.
I fear no one!
I'll never turn back and run
For Lord, you surround and protect me.
2When evil ones come to destroy me
They will be the ones who turn back.
3My heart will not be afraid
Even if an army rises to attack.
I know that you are there for me
So I will not be shaken.
4Here's the one thing I crave from God,
The one thing I seek above all else:
I want the privilege of living with him
Every moment in his house,
Finding the sweet loveliness of his face;
Filled with awe, delighting in his glory and grace.
I want to live my life so close to him
That he takes pleasure in my every prayer.
5-6In his shelter in the day of trouble,
That's where you'll find me,
For he hides me there in his holiness.
He has smuggled me into his secret place
Where I'm kept safe and secure—
Out of reach from all my enemies.
Triumphant now, I'll bring him my offerings of praise,

a Inscription from the Septuagint.
b 27:1 See also John 1:5, 9, and 1 John 1:5.

Singing and shouting with ecstatic joy!
Yes, listen and you can hear the fanfare
Of my shouts of praise to the Lord!
7God, hear my cry! Show me your grace,
Show me mercy, and send the help I need!
8Lord, when you said to me, "Seek my face,"
My inner being responded:
I'm seeking your face with all my heart.
9So don't hide yourself, Lord,
When I come to find you.
You're the God of my salvation;
How can you reject your servant in anger?
You've been my only hope,
So don't forsake me now when I need you!
10My father and mother abandoned me.
I'm like an orphan!
But you took me in and made me yours.[a]
11Now teach me all about your ways
And tell me what to do.
Make it clear for me to understand
For I am surrounded by waiting enemies.
12Don't let them defeat me, Lord.
You can't let me fall into their clutches!
They keep accusing me of things
I've never done, while they plot evil against me.
13Yet, I totally trust you to rescue me
One more time, so that I can see once again
How good you are while I'm still alive!
14Here's what I've learned through it all:
Don't give up, don't be impatient,
Be entwined as one with the Lord.[b]
Be brave, courageous, and never lose hope.
Yes, keep on waiting—
For he will never disappoint you!

a 27:10 Every child needs four things: acceptance, focused attention, guidance, and protection. All four of these emotional needs are met by God (verses 7–14).
b 27:14 Or, "wait upon the Lord." See Psalm 25:5 footnote.

Psalm 28

MY STRENGTH AND SHIELD

David's poetic praise to God

1I'm pleading with you, Lord, help me![a]
Don't close your ears to my cry, for you're my Defender.
If you continue to remain aloof and refuse to answer me
I might as well give up and die.
2Can't you see me turning toward your mercy seat,
As I lift my hands in surrendered prayer?
Now, Lord, please listen to my cry.
3Don't allow me to be punished along with the wicked;
These hypocrites who speak sweetly to their neighbor's face
While holding evil against them in their hearts.
4Go ahead and punish them as they deserve.
Let them be paid back for all their evil plans
In proportion to their wickedness.
5Since they don't care anything about you
Nor about the great things you've done,
Take them down like an old building being demolished,
Never again to be rebuilt.
6But may your name be blessed and built up!
For you have answered my passionate cry for mercy.
7You are my Strength and my Shield from every danger.
When I fully trust in you, help is on the way.
I jump for joy and burst forth with ecstatic, passionate praise!
I will sing songs of what you mean to me!
8You will be the inner strength of all your people,
The Mighty Protector of all;
The saving strength for all your anointed ones.
9Keep protecting and cherishing your chosen ones;
In you they will never fall.
Like a Shepherd going before us, keep leading us forward,
Forever carrying us in your arms!

a 28:1 This Psalm was likely written when David was exiled because of the rebellion of his son, Absalom. He was not longing and looking for his throne, but for God's throne (verse 2).

Psalm 29

THE GLORY-GOD THUNDERS!

King David's poetic praise to God for the last days
The Feast of Tabernacles[a]

1Proclaim his majesty all you mighty champions,
You sons of Almighty God,
Giving all the glory and strength back to him!
2Be in awe before his majesty.
Be in awe before such power and might!
Come worship wonderful Yahweh
Arrayed in all his splendor,
Bowing in worship as he appears in all his holy beauty.
Give him the honor due his name!
Worship him wearing the glory-garments
Of your holy, priestly calling!
3-4The voice of the Lord echoes through the skies and seas.
The Glory-God reigns as he thunders in the clouds.
So powerful is his voice, so brilliant and bright;
How majestic as he thunders over the great waters![b]
5His tympanic thunder topples the strongest of trees.[c]
His symphonic sound splinters the mighty forests.
6Now he moves Zion's[d] mountains by the might of his voice,[e]
Shaking the snowy peaks with his earsplitting sound!
7The lightning-fire flashes, striking as he speaks.
8God reveals himself when he makes the fault lines quake,
Shaking deserts, speaking his voice.
9God's mighty voice makes the deer to give birth.

a The additional words of the inscription are found in the Septuagint. Psalm 29 is one of the loveliest poems ever written. It is pure and unrestrained praise. The name *Yahweh* (Jehovah) is found eighteen times in eleven verses. David was a prophetic seer, and this Psalm can properly be interpreted to speak of God's majesty revealed in the last days.
b 29:3-4 The sea (great waters) is often a term used in the Bible to symbolize the "sea of humanity." See Isaiah 57:20 and Revelation 17:15.
c 29:5 Trees in the Bible are symbols used for men. The strongest of men are toppled and bowed down when the Glory-God speaks.
d 29:6 Or, "Sirion" (Mt. Hermon), an ancient term for Mount Zion. See Psalm 133.
e 29:6 The "voice of the Lord" is used seven times (the seven thunders) in this Psalm.

His thunderbolt voice lays the forest bare.
In his temple all fall before him
With each one shouting,
"Glory, glory, the God of glory!"[a]
10Above the furious flood,[b]
The Enthroned One reigns,
The King-God rules with eternity at his side.
11This is the One who gives
His strength and might to his people.
This is the Lord giving us his kiss of peace.[c]

a 29:9 The Septuagint reads, "Those who give him glory he carries to his house."

b 29:10 The Hebrew word for flood is found thirteen times in the Bible and is always used in connection to man's rebellion and turning away from God. Thirteen is the Biblical number signifying apostasy. Sitting as king, he rules even over the dark flood of evil to make it end.

c 29:11 In Jewish synagogues this Psalm is read on the first day of the feast of Pentecost. The Christian Church was born on Pentecost two thousand years ago when the mighty "storm" of the Spirit came into the upper room. See Acts 2. The last word of this Psalm is peace. It begins with a storm, but God brings his people peace even in the midst of storms.

Psalm 30

HE HEALED ME

King David's poetic praise to God
A song for the Feast of Dedication of the dwelling place

1Lord, I will exalt you and lift you high,
For you have lifted me up on high!
Over all my boasting, gloating enemies, you made me to triumph.
2O Lord, my healing God, I cried out for a miracle and you healed me!
3You brought me back from the brink of death, from the depths below.
Now here I am, alive and well, fully restored!
4O sing and make melody, you steadfast lovers of God,
Give thanks to him every time you reflect on his holiness!
5I've learned that his anger is short-lived,
But his loving favor lasts a lifetime![a]
We may weep through the night,
But at daybreak it will turn into shouts of ecstatic joy.
6-7I remember boasting, "I've got it made! Nothing can stop me now!
I'm God's favored one; he's made me steady as a mountain!"
But then suddenly, you hid your face from me.
I was panic-stricken and became so depressed.
8Still I cried out to you, Lord God, I shouted out for mercy, saying:
9"What would you gain in my death, if I were to go down
To the depths of darkness? Will a grave sing your song?
How could death's dust declare your faithfulness?"
10So hear me now, Lord, show me your famous mercy.
O God, be my Savior and rescue me!
11Then he broke through and transformed all my wailing
Into a whirling dance of ecstatic praise!
He has torn the veil and lifted from me
The sad heaviness of mourning.
He wrapped me in the glory-garments of gladness.

a 30:5 The Septuagint says, "There is wrath in his anger but life in his will [promise]."

12How could I be silent when it's time to praise you?
Now my heart sings out loud, bursting with joy–
A bliss inside that keeps me singing,
"I can never thank you enough!"

Psalm 31

HOW GREAT IS YOUR GOODNESS

For the Pure and Shining One
A song of poetic praise by King David

1 I trust you Lord, to be my Hiding Place.
Don't let me down.
Don't let my enemies bring me to shame.
Come and rescue me,
For you are the only God
Who always does what is right.
2 Rescue me quickly when I cry out to you.
At the sound of my prayer may your ear be turned to me.
Be my strong Shelter and Hiding Place on high.
Pull me into victory and breakthrough.
3-4 For you are my high Fortress where I'm kept safe.
You are to me a stronghold of salvation.
When you deliver me out of this peril
It will bring glory to your name.
As you guide me forth I'll be kept safe
From the hidden snares of the enemy,
The secret traps that lie before me,
For you have become my Rock of Strength.
5 Into your hands I now entrust my spirit.[a]
O Lord, the God of faithfulness,
You have rescued and redeemed me.
6 I despise these deceptive illusions,
All this pretense and nonsense;
For I worship only you.
7 In mercy you have seen my troubles,
And you have cared for me;
Even during this crisis in my soul I will be radiant with joy,
Filled with praise for your love and mercy.

a 31:5 This was quoted by Jesus as he was dying on the cross. See Matthew 27:50.

[8]You have kept me from being conquered by my enemy;
You broke open the way to bring me to freedom,[a]
Into a beautiful broad place.[b]
[9]O Lord, help me again! Keep showing me such mercy.
For I am in anguish, always in tears,
And I'm worn-out with weeping.
I'm becoming old because of grief, my health is broken.
[10]I'm exhausted! My life is spent with sorrow,
My years with sighing and sadness.
Because of all these troubles I have no more strength.
My inner being[c] is so weak and frail.
[11]My enemies say, "You are nothing!"
Even my friends and neighbors hold me in contempt!
They dread seeing me
And they look the other way when I pass by.
[12]I am totally forgotten, buried away like a dead man,
Discarded like a broken dish thrown in the trash.
[13]I overheard their whispered threats,
The slander of my enemies.
I'm terrified as they plot and scheme to take my life.
[14]I'm desperate, Lord! I throw myself upon you,
For you alone are my God!
[15]My life, my every moment,
My destiny—it's all in your hands.
So I know you can deliver me
From those who persecute me relentlessly.
[16]Let your shining face shine on me.
Let your undying love
And glorious grace save me
From all this gloom.
[17]As I call upon you let my shame and disgrace

Be replaced by your favor once again.
But let shame and disgrace fall instead upon the wicked,
Those going to their own doom,

a 31:8 This is a picture of the stone rolled away from the tomb of Jesus.
b 31:8 This could be the throne room where Jesus ascended after his death.
c 31:10 The Hebrew text says, "My bones grow weak." Bones in the Bible are symbols of our inner being.

Drifting down in silence to the dust of death.
18 At last their lying lips will be muted in their graves.
For they are arrogant,
Filled with contempt and conceit,
As they speak against the godly.
19 Lord, how wonderful you are!
You have stored up so many good things for us,
Like a treasure chest heaped up
And spilling over with blessings—
All for those who honor and worship you!
And everybody knows what you can do,
For those who turn and hide themselves in you.
20 So, hide all your beloved ones in the sheltered,
Secret place before your face.
Overshadow them by your glory-presence.
Keep them from these accusations,
The brutal insults of evil men.
Tuck them safely away in the
Tabernacle where you dwell.
21 The name of the Lord is blessed and lifted high!
For his marvelous miracle of mercy protected me
When I was overwhelmed by my enemies.
22 I spoke so hastily when I said, "The Lord has deserted me."
For in truth, you did hear my prayer and came to rescue me.
23 Listen to me all you godly ones: Love the Lord with passion!
The Lord protects and preserves all those who are loyal to him.
But he pays back in full all those who reject him in their pride.
24 So cheer up! Take courage all you who love him!
Wait for him to break through for you, all who trust in him!

Psalm 32

FORGIVEN

A poem of insight and instruction by King David [a]

1How happy and fulfilled are those
Whose rebellion has been forgiven,[b]
Those whose sins are covered by blood![c]
2How blessed and relieved are those
Who have confessed their corruption[d] to God!
For he wipes their slates clean
And removes hypocrisy from their hearts.
3Before I confessed my sins, I kept it all inside;
My dishonesty devastated my inner life,
Causing my life to be filled with frustration,
Irrepressible anguish, and misery.
4The pain never let up, for your hand of conviction
Was heavy on my heart.
My strength was sapped,
My inner life dried up
Like a spiritual drought within my soul.

Pause in his presence

5Then I finally admitted to you all my sins,
Refusing to hide them any longer.
So I said, "My life-giving God,
I'll openly acknowledge my evil actions."
And you forgave me!
All at once the guilt of my sin washed away,
And all my pain disappeared!

Pause in his presence

a David wrote this Psalm after he seduced the wife of his most loyal soldier, then had him killed to try to keep her pregnancy a secret. This sin with Bathsheba brought great disgrace to David, yet he finds complete forgiveness in God's mercy. The apostle Paul chose the first two verses of Psalm 32 to support the important doctrine of salvation by grace through faith. See Romans 4:5–8. This was Saint Augustine's favorite psalm. He had it written on the wall near his bed before he died so he could meditate upon it.

b 32:1 The Hebrew word for *forgiven* means lifted off. Sin's guilt is a burden that must be lifted off our souls. The Septuagint says, "because they have not hidden their sins."

c 32:1 Implied in the text.

d 32:2 David uses three Hebrew words to describe sin in these first two verses: *rebellion, sins* (failures, falling short), and *corruption* (crookedness, the twisting of right standards).

6This is what I've learned through it all:
Every believer should confess their sins to God;
Do it every time God has uncovered you,
In the time of exposing.
For if you do this,
When sudden storms of life overwhelm,
You'll be kept safe.[a]
7Lord, You are my secret Hiding Place,
Protecting me from these troubles,
Surrounding me with songs of gladness!
Your joyous shouts of rescue
Release my breakthrough.

Pause in his presence

8-9I hear the Lord saying, "I will stay close to you,
Instructing and guiding you
Along the pathway for your life.
I will advise you along the way,
And lead you forth with my eyes as your guide.
So don't make it difficult, don't be stubborn
When I take you where you've not been before.
Don't make me tug you and pull you along.
Just come with me!"
10So my conclusion is this:
Many are the sorrows and frustrations
Of those who don't come clean with God.
But when you trust in the Lord for forgiveness,
His wrap-around love will surround you.
11So celebrate the goodness of God!
He shows this kindness to everyone who is his!
Go ahead—shout for joy,
All you upright ones who want to please him!

a 32:6 Proverbs 2:13 is a good commentary on this verse.

Psalm 33

A SONG OF PRAISE

Poetic praise by King David[a]

[1]It's time to sing and shout for joy!
Go ahead all you redeemed ones, do it!
Praise him with all you have,
For praise looks lovely on the lips of God's lovers.
[2]Play the guitar as you lift your praises loaded with thanksgiving.
Sing and make joyous music with all you've got inside.
[3]Compose new melodies[b] that release new praises to the Lord.
Play his praises on instruments
With the anointing and skill he gives you.
Sing and shout with passion,
Make a spectacular sound of joy—
[4]For God's Word is something to sing about!
He is true to his promises; his Word can be trusted;
And everything he does is so reliable and right.
[5]The Lord loves seeing justice on the earth.
Anywhere and everywhere
You can find his faithful, unfailing love!
[6]All he had to do was speak
By his Spirit-Wind command,
And God created the heavenlies,
Filled with galaxies and stars,
The vast cosmos he wonderfully made.
[7]His voice scooped out the seas.
The ocean depths he poured into vast reservoirs.
[8]Now, with breathtaking wonder,
Let everyone worship Yahweh, this awe-inspiring Creator.
[9]Words he breathed and worlds were birthed,

a Most manuscripts have no inscription for this Psalm. However, ancient Qumran evidence suggests this is the original inscription that was later omitted.

b 33:3 There are seven new songs mentioned in the Bible. Six are in the Psalms (33:3, 40:3, 96:1, 98:1, 144:9, 149:1) and one in Isaiah (42:10).

"Let there be" and there it was—
Springing forth the moment he spoke.
No sooner said than done!
10With his breath he scatters
The schemes of nations who oppose him;
They will never succeed.
11His destiny-plan for the earth stands sure.
His forever-plan remains in place and will never fail.
12Blessed and prosperous
Is that nation who has God as their Lord!
They will be the people he chooses for his own.
13-15The Lord looks over us from where he rules in heaven.
Gazing into every heart from his lofty dwelling place,
He observes all the peoples of the earth.
The Creator of our hearts
Considers and examines everything we do.
16Even if a king has the best equipped army
It would never be enough to save him.
Even if the best warrior went to battle
He could not be saved simply by his strength alone.
17Human strength and the weapons of man
Are such false hopes for victory;
They may seem mighty but they will always disappoint.
18The eyes of the Lord are upon
Even the weakest worshippers who love him,[a]
Those who wait in hope and expectation
For the strong, steady love of God.
19God will deliver them from death,
Even the certain death of famine, with no one to help.
20The Lord alone is our radiant hope
And we trust in him with all our hearts.
His wraparound presence will strengthen us.
21As we trust, we rejoice with an uncontained joy,
Flowing from Yahweh!
22So let your love and steadfast kindness overshadow us
Continually—for we trust and we wait upon you!

a 33:18 Implied in the text.

Psalm 34

GOD'S GOODNESS

A song by King David composed after his escape
from the king when he pretended to be insane

1Lord! I'm bursting with joy over what you've done for me!
My lips are full of perpetual praise.
2I'm boasting of you and all your works,
So let all who are discouraged take heart.
3Join me everyone! Let's praise the Lord together.
Let's make him famous!
Let's make his name glorious to all.
4So listen to my testimony: I cried to God in my distress
And he answered me! He freed me from all my fears!
5Gaze upon him, join your life with his, and joy will come.
Your faces will glisten with glory.
You'll never wear that shame-face again.
6When I had nothing—desperate and defeated,
I cried out to the Lord and he heard me,
Bringing his miracle-deliverance when I needed it most.[a]
7The angels stooped down to listen as I prayed,
Encircling me, empowering me, and showing me how to escape.
They will do this for everyone who fears God.
8Drink deeply of the pleasures of this God.[b]
Experience for yourself the joyous mercies he gives
To all who turn to hide themselves in him.
9Worship in awe and wonder, all you who've been made holy!
For all who fear him will feast with plenty.
10Even the strong and the wealthy[c] grow weak and hungry,
But those who passionately pursue the Lord

a 34:6 David wrote this Psalm at perhaps the lowest point in his life. He was alone. He had to part from Jonathan, his dearest friend. He was being chased by Saul and his paid assassins. Now he had run to hide in the cave of Adullam ("their prey"). Yet the beautiful sounds of praise were heard echoing in his cavern. This is a lesson for all of us: we praise our way out of our difficulties into his light.

b 34:8 Many translations read, "Taste and see." The Hebrew root word for see is taken from a word that means,to drink deeply.

c 34:10 Following the ancient versions (Septuagint, Syriac, and Vulgate), this phrase is translated "rich ones." Modern translations read "young lions."

Will never lack any good thing.
11Come, children of God, and listen to me.
I'll share the lesson I've learned of fearing the Lord.
12-13Do you want to live a long, good life,
Enjoying the beauty that fills each day?
Then never speak a lie
Or allow wicked words to come from your mouth.[a]
14Keep turning your back on every sin,
And make "peace" your life motto.
Practice being at peace with everyone.
15The Lord sees all we do;
He watches over his friends day and night.
His godly ones receive the answers they seek,
Whenever they cry out to him.
16But the Lord has made up his mind to oppose evildoers
And to wipe out even the memory of them
From the face of the earth.
17Yet when holy lovers of God cry out
To him with all their hearts, the Lord will hear them
And come to rescue them from all their troubles.
18The Lord is so close to all whose hearts are crushed by pain,
And he is always ready to restore the repentant one.
19Even when bad things happen to the good and godly ones,
The Lord will save them and not let them be defeated
By what they face.
20God will be your bodyguard to protect you
When trouble is near. Not one bone will be broken.
21But the wicked commit slow suicide.
For they hate and persecute the lovers of God.
Make no mistake about it,
God will hold them guilty and punish them;
They will pay the penalty!
22But the Lord has paid for the freedom of his servants,
And he will freely pardon those who love him.
He will declare them free and innocent
When they turn to hide themselves in him.

a 34:12-13 See 1 Peter 3:10-12.

Psalm 35

RESCUE ME

A poetic song by King David[a]

Part One – David, a Warrior

1O Lord, fight for me! Harass the hecklers, accuse my accusers.
Fight those who fight against me.
2-3Put on your armor, Lord; take up your shield and protect me.
Rise up, mighty God! Grab your weapons of war
And block the way of the wicked who come to fight me.
Stand for me when they stand against me!
Speak over my soul: "I am your strong Savior!"[b]
4Humiliate those who seek my harm. Defeat them all!
Frustrate their plans to defeat me and drive them back.
Disgrace them all as they have devised their plans to disgrace me.
5Blow them away like dust in the wind,
With the Angel of Almighty God driving them back!
6And make the road in front of them nothing but slippery darkness,
With the Angel of the Lord behind them chasing them away!
7For though I did nothing wrong to them they set a trap for me,
Wanting me to fall and fail.
8Surprise them with your ambush, Lord,
And catch them in the very trap they set for me.
Let them be the ones to fail and fall into destruction!
9And then my fears will dissolve into limitless joy;
My whole being will overflow with gladness
Because of your mighty deliverance.
10Everything inside of me will shout it out:
"There's just no one like you, Lord!"
For look at how you protect the weak and helpless
From the strong and heartless who oppress them.

a This is the first of seven Psalms in which David cried out for vengeance upon his enemies (Psalms 52, 58, 59, 69, 109, and 137).

b 35:2–3 The Aramaic word used here is found thirty-three times in the Psalms, and is clearly *Savior*. Although a New Testament concept, David had a deep understanding almost one thousand years before the Savior was born that God would become his Savior. The Hebrew word for *Savior*, *Yasha*, is very similar to the name *Jesus*, *Yeshua*.

Part Two – David, a Witness

11They are malicious men, hostile witnesses of wrong.
They rise up against me,
Accusers appearing out of nowhere.
12When I show them mercy they bring me misery.
I'm forsaken and forlorn, like a motherless child.
13I even prayed over them when they were sick.
I was burdened and bowed low with fasting
And interceded for their healing,
And I didn't stop praying.
14I grieved for them, heavyhearted,
As though they were my dearest family members
Or my good friends who were sick,
Nearing death, needing prayer.
15But when I was the one who tripped up and stumbled,
They came together only to slander me,
Rejoicing in my time of trouble, tearing me to shreds
With their lies and betrayal.
16These nameless ruffians,
Mocking me like godless fools at a feast—
How they delight in throwing mud on my name.
17God, how long can you just stand there doing nothing?
Now is the time to act.
Rescue me from these brutal men,
For I am being torn to shreds by these "beasts"
Who are out to get me.
Save me from their rage, their cruel grasp.
18 For then I will praise you wherever I go.[a]
And when everyone gathers for worship,
I will lift up your praise with a shout
In front of the largest crowd I can find!

Part Three – David, a Worshipper

19Don't let those who fight me for no reason be victorious.
Don't let them succeed, these heartless haters

a 35:18 The Septuagint says, "My only child, I will save you from the lions."

Who come against me with their gloating sneers.
20They are the ones who would never seek peace as friends,
For they are ever devising deceit against the innocent ones
Who mind their own business.
21They open their mouths with ugly grins,
Gloating with glee over my every fault.
"Look," they say, "we caught him red-handed!
We saw him fall with our own eyes!"
22But my caring God, you have been there all along.
You have seen their hypocrisy.
God, don't let them get away with this.
Don't walk away without doing something.
23Now is the time to awake! Rise up, Lord!
Vindicate me, my Lord and my God!
24You have every right to judge me, Lord,
According to your righteousness,
But don't let them rejoice over me when I stumble.
25-26Let them all be ashamed of themselves,
Humiliated when they rejoice over my every blunder.
Shame them, Lord, when they say, "We saw what he did.
Now we have him right where we want him.
Let's get him while he's down!"
Make them look ridiculous
When they exalt themselves over me.
May they all be disgraced and dishonored!
27But let all my true friends shout for joy,
All those who know and love what I do for you.
Let them all say, "The Lord will be glorified through it all!
God will still bless his servant!"
28Then I won't be able to hold it in—
Everyone will hear my joyous praises all day long!
Your righteousness will be the theme of my glory-song of praise!

Psalm 36

THE BLESSING OF THE WISE

A poetic song by King David, the servant of the Lord

1The rebellion of sin speaks as an oracle of God;
Speaking deeply to the conscience of wicked men.[a]
Yet they are still eager to sin,[b]
For the fear of God is not before their eyes.
2See how they flatter themselves,
Unable to detect and detest their sins.
They are crooked and conceited,
Convinced they can get away with anything.
3Their wicked words are nothing but lies.
Wisdom is far from them.
Goodness is both forgotten and forsaken.
4They lay awake at night to hatch their evil plots,
Always planning their schemes of darkness,
And never once do they consider the evil of their ways.
5But you, O Lord, your mercy-seat love is limitless,
Reaching higher than the highest heavens.
Your great faithfulness is so infinite,
Stretching over the whole earth.
6Your righteousness is unmovable,
Just like the mighty mountains.
Your judgments are as full of wisdom
As the oceans are full of water.
Your tender care and kindness
Leave no one forgotten,
Not a man nor even a mouse.
7O God, how extravagant is your cherishing love!
All mankind can find a hiding place,
Under the shadow of your wings.

a 36:1 Or, "the heart of the wicked is rebellious to the core."
b 36:1 Implied in the text.

8All may drink of the anointing[a]
From the abundance of your house!
All may drink their fill
From the delightful springs of Eden.[b]
9To know you is to experience a Flowing Fountain,
Drinking in your life, springing up to satisfy.
In the light of your holiness
We receive the light of revelation.[c]
10Lord, keep pouring out your unfailing love
On those who are near you.
Release more of your blessings
To those who are loyal to you.
11Don't let these proud boasters trample me down;
Don't let them push me around
By the sheer strength of their wickedness.
12There they lie in the dirt, these evil ones
Thrown down to the ground,
Never to arise again!

a 36:8 The Hebrew word for *abundance* is actually *butterfat* or *oil*. It is a symbol of the anointing of the Holy Spirit.
b 36:8 Or, "Eden's rivers of pleasure." The garden of Eden had flowing rivers of delight. Eden means *pleasure*. The Hebrew word used here is the plural form of Eden, *Edens*.
c 36:9 See John 1:4.

Psalm 37

A SONG OF WISDOM

Poetic praise by King David[a]

1Don't follow after the wicked ones,
Or be jealous of their wealth.
Don't think for a moment they're better-off than you.
2They and their short-lived success[b]
Will soon shrivel up and quickly fade away
Like grass clippings in the hot sun.
3Keep trusting in the Lord and do what is right in his eyes.
Fix your heart on the promises of God and you will be secure,
Feasting on his faithfulness.
4Make God the utmost delight and pleasure of your life,[c]
And he will provide for you what you desire the most.
5Give God the right to direct your life,[d]
And as you trust him along the way
You'll find he pulled it off perfectly!
6He will appear as your Righteousness,[e]
As sure as the dawning of a new day.
He will manifest as your Justice,
As sure and strong as the noonday sun.
7Quiet your heart in his presence and pray;
Keep hope alive as you long for God to come through for you,
And don't think for a moment
That the wicked in their prosperity
Are better-off than you.
8Stay away from anger and revenge.
Keep envy far from you, for it only leads you into lies.
9For one day the wicked will be destroyed,

a Psalm 37 is an acrostic Psalm with every other verse beginning with a successive letter of the Hebrew alphabet.
b 37:2 Implied in the text.
c 37:4 The word *delight* actually means to be soft or tender.
d 37:5 The Hebrew uses the word *commit*, which means "to roll over your burdens on the Lord."
e 37:6 The Hebrew verb found here is also used for giving birth. Perhaps this is a reference to the birth of Christ, our Righteousness.

But those who trust in the Lord
Will live safe and sound with blessings overflowing.
10Just a little while longer and the ungodly will vanish;
You will look for them in vain.
11But the humble of heart will inherit every promise[a]
And enjoy abundant peace.
12Let the wicked keep plotting against the godly
With all their sneers and arrogant jeers.
13God doesn't lose any sleep over them
And he knows their day is coming!
14Evil ones take aim on the poor and helpless;
They are ready to slaughter those who do right.
15But the Lord will intervene[b]
And turn all their weapons of wickedness back on themselves,
Piercing their pride-filled hearts until they are the helpless.
16It is so much better to have little,
Combined with much of God,
Than to have the fabulous wealth of the wicked
And nothing else.
17For the Lord takes care of all his forgiven ones
While the strength of the evil will surely slip away.
18Day by day the Lord watches the good deeds of the godly
And he prepares for them his forever-reward.
19Even in a time of disaster he will watch over them,
And they will always have more than enough
No matter what happens.
20All the enemies of God will perish.
For the wicked have only a momentary value, a fading glory.
Then one day they vanish! Here today, gone tomorrow.
21They break their promises, borrowing money
But never paying it back.
The good man returns what he owes
With some extra besides.
22The Lord's blessed ones receive it all in the end,
But the cursed ones will be cut off

a 37:11 Jesus said it this way: "The meek will inherit the earth." See Matthew 5:5.
b 37:15 Implied in the text.

With nothing to show for themselves.
23The steps of the God-pursuing ones
Follow firmly in the footsteps of the Lord.
And God delights in every step they take to follow him.
24If they stumble badly they will still survive,
For the Lord lifts them up with his hands.
25I was once young, but now I'm old.
Not once have I found a lover of God forsaken by him,
Nor have any of their children gone hungry.
26Instead, I've found the godly ones
To be the generous ones who give freely to others.
Their children are blessed and become a blessing.
27If you truly want to dwell forever in God's presence
Then forsake evil and do what is right in his eyes.
28The Lord loves it when he sees us walking in his justice.
He will never desert his devoted lovers;
They will be kept forever in his faithful care.
But the descendants of the wicked will be banished.
29The faithful lovers of God will inherit the earth
And enjoy every promise of God's care;
Dwelling in peace forever.
30God-lovers make the best counselors.
Their words possess wisdom
And are right and trustworthy.
31The ways of God are in their hearts
And they won't swerve from
The paths of steadfast righteousness.
32Evil ones spy on the godly ones, stalking them
To find something they could use to accuse them.
They're out for the kill!
33But God will foil all their plots.
The godly will not stand condemned when brought to trial.
34So don't be impatient for the Lord to act;
Keep moving forward steadily in his ways,
And he will exalt you at the right time.[a]

a 37:34 Implied in the text.

And when he does, you will possess every promise,
Including your full inheritance.
You'll watch with your own eyes
And see the wicked lose everything.
35I've already seen this happen.
Once I saw a wicked and violent man
Overpower all who were around him,
A domineering tyrant with
His pride and oppressive ways.
36Then he died and was forgotten.
Now no one cares that he is gone forever.
37But you can tell who are the blameless
And spiritually mature.
What a different story with them![a]
The godly ones will have a peaceful, prosperous future
With a happy ending.
38Every evil sinner will be destroyed, obliterated.
They'll be utter failures with no future!
39But the Lord will be the Savior of all who love him.
Even in their time of trouble
God will live in them as Strength.
40Because of their faith in him, their daily portion will be
A Father's help, and deliverance from evil.
This is true for all who turn to hide themselves in him!

a 37:37 Implied in the context.

Psalm 38

A GROAN BEFORE THE THRONE

A poetic lament to remember by King David[a]

1O Lord, don't punish me angrily for what I've done.
Don't let my sin inflame your wrath against me.
2For the arrows of your conviction
Have pierced me so deeply.
Your blows have struck my soul and crushed me.
3Now my body is sick.
My health is totally broken because of your anger,
And it's all due to my sins!
4I'm overwhelmed, swamped, and submerged
Beneath the heavy burden of my guilt.
It clings to me and won't let me go.
5My rotting wounds are a witness against me.
They are severe and getting worse;
Reminding me of my failure and folly.
6I am completely broken because of what I've done.
Gloom is all around me.
My sins have bent me over to the ground.
7-8My inner being is shriveled up;
My self-confidence crushed.
Sick with fever I'm left exhausted.
Now I'm cold as a corpse
And nothing is left inside of me
But great groaning filled with anguish.
9Lord, you know all my desires and deepest longings.
My tears are liquid words
And you can read them all.
10-11My heart beats wildly, my strength is sapped,
And the light of my eyes is going out.
My friends stay far away from me,

a The Septuagint has in the inscription: "To be remembered on the Sabbath."

Avoiding me like the plague.
Even my family wants nothing to do with me.
12Meanwhile my enemies are out to kill me,
Plotting my ruin, speaking of my doom
As they spend every waking moment
Planning on how to finish me off.
13-14I'm like a deaf man who no longer hears.
I can't even speak up, and words fail me;
I have no argument to counter their threats.
15Lord, the only thing I can do is wait
And put my hope in you.
I wait for your help, my God.
16So hear my cry and put an end
To their strutting in pride;
Who gloat when I stumble in pain.
17I'm slipping away and on the verge of a breakdown,
With nothing but sorrow and sighing.[a]
18I confess all my sin to you;
I can't hold it in any longer.
My agonizing thoughts punish me for my wrongdoing;
I feel condemned as I consider all I've done.
19My enemies are many.
They hate me and persecute me,
Though I've done nothing against them to deserve it.
20I show goodness to them
And get repaid evil in return.
And they hate me even more
When I stand for what is right.
21So don't forsake me now, Lord!
Don't leave me in this condition.
22God, hurry to help me, run to my rescue!
For you're my Savior and my only hope!

a 38:17 The Septuagint reads, "I am prepared for all of their whips—prepared to suffer."

Psalm 39

A CRY FOR HELP

For the Pure and Shining One
A song of praising by King David[a]

1-2Here's my life motto, the truth I live by:
I will guard my ways for all my days.
I will speak only what is right,
Guarding what I speak.
Like a watchman guards against an attack of the enemy,
I'll guard and muzzle my mouth
When the wicked are around me.
I will remain silent and will not grumble,
Or speak out of my disappointment.
But the longer I'm silent my pain grows worse!
3-4My heart burned with a fire within me,
And my thoughts eventually boiled over,
Until they finally came rolling out of my mouth—
"Lord, help me to know
How fleeting my time on earth is.
Help me to know how limited is my life
And that I'm only here but for a moment more.
5"What a brief time you've given me to live![b]
Compared to you my lifetime is nothing at all!
Nothing more than a puff of air,
I'm gone so swiftly.
And so too are the grandest of men;
They are nothing but a fleeting shadow!"

Pause in his presence

6We live our lives like those living in shadows.[c]
All our activities and energies are spent

a The Hebrew inscription includes the name *Jeduthun*, which can be translated praising.
b 39:5 Interestingly, the Hebrew word for *short* in this verse is "a handbreadth," or the span of a man's hand. Our life's duration is compared to a mere six-inch span!
c 39:6 Or, "like phantoms going to and fro."

For things that pass away.
We gather, we hoard,
We cling to our things,
Only to leave them all behind for who knows who.
7And now, God,[a] I'm left with one conclusion.
My only hope is to hope in you alone!
8Save me from being overpowered by my sin;
Don't make me a disgrace before the degenerate!
9Lord, I'm left speechless and I have no excuse,
So I'll not complain any longer.
Now I know you're the One who is behind it all.
10But I can't take it much longer.
Spare me these blows from your discipline-rod.
For if you are against me I will waste away to nothing.
11No one endures when you rebuke
And discipline us for our sins.
Like a cobweb is swept away with a wave of the hand,
You sweep away all that we once called dear.
How fleeting and frail our lives!
We're nothing more than a puff of air.

Pause in his presence

12Lord, listen to all my tender cries.
Read my every tear, like liquid words
That plead for your help.
I feel all alone at times, like a stranger to you
Passing through this life
Just like all those before me.
13Don't let me die without restoring
Joy and gladness to my soul.
May your frown over my failure
Become a smile over my success.

a 39:7 The Aramaic is *Maryah*, the Aramaic form of YHWH or Lord Jehovah.

Psalm 40

A JOYFUL SALVATION

For the Pure and Shining One
A song of poetic praise by King David

1 I waited and waited and waited some more;
Patiently, knowing God would come through for me.
Then, at last, he bent down and listened to my cry.
2 He stooped down to lift me out of danger,
From the desolate pit I was in,
Out of the muddy mess I had fallen into.
Now he's lifted me up into a firm, secure place,
And steadied me while I walk along his ascending path.
3 A new song for a new day rises up in me
Every time I think about how he breaks through for me!
Ecstatic praise pours out of my mouth until
Everyone hears how God has set me free.
Many will see his miracles; they'll stand in awe of God,
And fall in love with him!
4 Blessing after blessing comes to those
Who love and trust the Lord. They will not fall away,
For they refuse to listen to the lies of the proud.
5 O Lord, our God, no one can compare with you.
Such wonderful works and miracles are all found with you!
And you think of us all the time
With your countless expressions of love—
Far exceeding our expectations!
6 It's not sacrifices that really move your heart.
Burnt offerings, sin offerings—that's not what brings you joy.
But when you open my ears and speak deeply to me,
I become your willing servant, and a body you prepared for me.[a]

a 40:6 As translated from the Septuagint. The Hebrew says, "You have pierced my ear." This is a Hebraic reference to being a bond servant whose ear has been pierced by his master to signify a desire to serve for life. See Exodus 21:1–6, Isaiah 50:5, and Hebrews 10:5.

7So I said: "Here I am! I'm coming to you as a sacrifice,[a]
For in the prophetic scrolls of your book
You have written about me.
8I delight to fulfill your will, my God,
For your living words
Are written upon the pages of my heart."
9I tell everyone everywhere the truth of your righteousness.
And you know I haven't held back in telling the message to all.
10I don't keep it a secret, or hide the truth.
I preach of your faithfulness and kindness,
Proclaiming your extravagant love to the largest crowd I can find!
11So Lord, don't hold back your love or withhold
Your tender mercies from me.
Keep me in your truth and let your compassion overflow to me
No matter what I face.
12Evil surrounds me; problems greater than I can solve
Come one after another. Without you, I know I can't make it.
My sins are so many!
I'm so ashamed to lift my face to you.
For my guilt grabs me and stings my soul
Until I am weakened and spent.
13Please, Lord! Come quickly and rescue me!
Take pleasure in showing me your favor and restore me.
14Let all who seek my life be humiliated!
Let them be confused and ashamed, God—
Scatter those who wish me evil;
They just want me dead.
15Scoff at every scoffer and cause them all to be utter failures.
Let them be ashamed and horrified by their complete defeat.
16But let all who passionately seek you
Erupt with excitement and joy over what you've done!
Let all your lovers rejoice continually in the Savior,[b]
Saying: "How great and glorious is our God!"
17Lord, in my place of weakness and need, I ask again:

a 40:7 Implied in the context. See Hebrews 10:5–7.
b 40:16 This verse contains the root word for *Yeshua* in Hebrew.

Will you come and help me?
I know I'm always in your thoughts.
You are my true Savior and Hero,
So don't delay to deliver me now,
For you are my God.

Psalm 41

I NEED YOU, LORD

King David's poetic song for the Pure and Shining One

1God always blesses those who are
Kind to the poor and helpless.
They're the first ones God helps
When they find themselves in any trouble.
2The Lord will preserve and protect them.
They'll be honored and esteemed[a]
While their enemies are defeated.
3When they are sick, God will restore them,
Lying upon their bed of suffering.
He will raise them up again
And restore them back to health.
4So in my sickness I say to you,
"Lord, be my Kind Healer.
Heal my body and soul; heal me, God!
For I have confessed my sins to you."[b]
5But those who hate me wish the worst for me, saying,
"When will he die and be forgotten?"
6And when these "friends" come to visit me
With their pious sympathy,
And their hollow words
And with hypocrisy hidden in their hearts—
I can see right through it all. For they come
Merely to gather gossip about me,
Using all they find to mock me
With malicious hearts of slander.
7They are wicked whisperers
Who imagine the worst for me,
Repeating their rumors, saying:

a 41:2 Or, "they will be blessed in the land."
b 41:4 Implied in the context.

8"He got what he deserved; it's over for him!
The spirit of infirmity[a] is upon him and
He'll never get over this illness."
9Even my ally, my friend, has turned against me.
He was one I totally trusted with my life,
Sharing supper with him,[b]
And now he shows me nothing
But betrayal and treachery.
He has sold me as an enemy.[c]
10So Lord, please don't desert me when I need you!
Give me grace and get me back on my feet
So I can triumph over them all.
11Then I'll know you're pleased with me,
When you allow me to taste of victory over all my foes.
12Now stand up for me and don't let me fall,
For I've walked with integrity.
Keep me before your face forever.
13Everyone praise the Lord God of Israel,
Always and forever!
For he is from eternity past
And will remain for the eternity to come.
That's the way it will be forever!
Faithful is our King! Amen![d]

a 41:8 Or, "a thing of Belial," or, "an affliction from the abandoned one."
b 41:9 In the culture of that day, sharing a meal together was a sign of covenant friendship.
c 41:9 The Hebrew literally reads, "He lifted up his heel against me." This is a powerful figure of speech meaning he was sold as an enemy and was treated treacherously. This verse was quoted, in part, by Jesus at the Last Supper (John 13:18).
d 41:13 Some scholars believe this last verse was added as a "doxology of praise," marking the end of the first book of Psalms. The word *Amen* means "Faithful is our King!"

BOOK II

The "Exodus" Psalms

PSALMS OF SUFFERING AND REDEMPTION

Psalm 42

A CRY FOR REVIVAL[a]

For the Pure and Shining One
A contemplative poem for instruction by the prophetic singers of Korah's clan[b]

1 I long to drink of you, O God,
Drinking deeply from the streams of pleasure[c]
Flowing from your presence.
My longings overwhelm me for more of you![d]
2 My soul thirsts, pants, and longs for the Living God.
I want to come and see the face of God.
3 Day and night my tears keep falling
And my heart keeps crying for your help,
While my enemies mock me over and over, saying,
"Where is this god of yours? Why doesn't he help you?"[e]
4 So I speak over my heartbroken soul,
"Take courage. Remember when you used to be
Right out front leading the procession of praise
When the great crowd of worshippers
Gathered to go into the presence of the Lord?
You shouted with joy as the sound of passionate celebration
Filled the air and the joyous multitude of lovers
Honored the festival of the Lord!"
5 So then, my soul, why would you be depressed?
Why would you sink into despair?
Just keep hoping and waiting on God, your Savior.
For no matter what, I will still sing with praise,
For living before his face is my saving grace!
6 But here I am depressed and downcast.

a Psalms 42 and 43 were originally composed as one Psalm and later made into two.
b Korah was the great-grandson of Levi. The sons of Korah were a family of Levitical singers. David chose them to preside over the music of the tabernacle-tent on Mount Zion.
c 42:1 Implied in the context of the Psalms.
d 42:1 The literal Hebrew is "as the deer pants for streams of water." The translator has chosen to take the metaphor of a hunted deer and put it into terms that transfer the meaning into today's context.
e 42:3 Implied in the text.

Yet I will still remember you as I ponder the place
Where your glory streams down,
From the mighty mountaintops, lofty and majestic,
The mountains of your awesome presence.[a]
7My deep need calls out to the deep kindness of your love.
Your waterfall of weeping sent waves of sorrow
Over my soul, carrying me away,
Cascading over me like a thundering cataract.
8Yet all day long God's promises of love pour over me.
Through the night I sing his songs,
For my prayer to God has become my life.
9I will say to God, "You are my Mountain of Strength;
How could you forget me? Why must I suffer
This vile oppression of my enemies,
These heartless tormentors who are out to kill me?"
10Their wounding words pierce my heart,
Over and over while they say,
"Where is this god of yours?"
11So I say to my soul, "Don't be discouraged,
Don't be disturbed, for I know
My God will break through for me."
Then I'll have plenty of reasons
To praise him all over again.
Yes, living before his face is my saving grace!

a 42:6 Implied in the context. The Hebrew text contains *Mount Hermon* and *Mount Mizar*, considered to be sacred mountains in the Hebrew culture. *Hermon* means lofty and majestic.

Psalm 43

LIGHT AND TRUTH

For the Pure and Shining One by the prophetic singers of Korah's clan[a]
A contemplative poem for instruction

1God, clear my name. Plead my case
Against the unjust charges
Of these ungodly workers of wickedness.
Deliver me from these lying degenerates.
2For you are where my strength comes from[b]
And my Protector,[c]
So why would you leave me now?
Must I be covered with gloom
While the enemy comes after me gloating with glee?
3Pour into me the brightness of your daybreak!
Pour into me your rays of revelation-truth!
Let them comfort and gently lead me onto the shining path,
Showing the way into your burning presence,
Into your many sanctuaries of holiness.
4Then I will come closer to your very altar
Until I come before you, the God of my ecstatic joy!
I will praise you with the harp that plays in my heart,
To you, my God, my magnificent God!
5Then I will say to my soul,
"Don't be discouraged, don't be disturbed,
For I fully expect my Savior-God to break through for me.
Then I'll have plenty of reasons
To praise him all over again."
Yes, living before his face is my saving grace!

a Although there is no inscription for this Psalm, it was originally part of Psalm 42.
b 43:2 Or, "God of my strength."
c 43:2 Implied in the text.

Psalm 44

WAKE UP, LORD, WE'RE IN TROUBLE

For the Pure and Shining One by the prophetic singers of Korah's clan
A contemplative poem for instruction

[The Past]

1-2God, we've heard about all the glorious miracles
You've done for our ancestors in days gone by.
They told us about the ancient times how by your power
You drove out the ungodly nations from this land,
Crushing all their strongholds, and giving the land to us.
Now the people of Israel cover the land from one end to the other,
All because of your grace and power![a]
3Our forefathers didn't win these battles
By their own strength, or their own skill or strategy.
But it was through the shining forth of your radiant-presence
And the display of your mighty power.
You loved to give them victory,
For you took great delight in them.
4You are my God, my King!
It's now time to decree majesties for Israel![b]
5Through your glorious name and your awesome power
We can push through to any victory and defeat every enemy.
6For I will not trust in the weapons of the world;[c]
I know they will never save me.
7Only you will be our Savior from all our enemies.
All those who hate us you have brought to shame.
8So now I constantly boast in you. I can never thank you enough!

Pause in his presence

a 44:1-2 Implied in the context.
b 44:4 Or, "Jacob."
c 44:6 Or, "bow and sword."

[The Present]

9But you have turned your back on us; you walked off and left us!
You've rejected us; tossing us aside in humiliating shame.
You don't go before us anymore in our battles.
10We retreat before our enemies in defeat,
For you are no longer helping us. Those who hate us
Have invaded our land and plundered our people.
11You have treated us like sheep in the slaughter pen,
Ready to be butchered. You've scattered us to the four winds.
12You have sold us as slaves for nothing!
You have counted us, your precious ones, as worthless.
13You have caused our neighbors to despise and scorn us.
All that are around us mock and curse us.
14You have made us the butt of their jokes.
Disliked by all, we are the laughingstock of the people.
15-16There's no escape from this constant curse, this humiliation!
We are despised, jeered, overwhelmed by shame,
And overcome at every turn by our hateful and heartless enemies.
17Despite all of this, we have not forgotten you;
We have not broken covenant with you.
18We have not betrayed you; our hearts are still yours.
Our steps have not strayed from your path.
19Yet you have crushed us, leaving us
In this wilderness place of misery and desperation.[a]
With nowhere else to turn,
Death's dark door seems to be the only way out.[b]
20-21If we had forsaken your holy name, wouldn't you know it?
You'd be right in leaving us. If we had worshipped before other gods,
No one would blame you for punishing us.
God, you know our every heart-secret.
You know we still want you![c]
22Because of you we face death threats every day,
Like martyrs we are dying daily! We are seen as lambs
Lined up to be slaughtered as sacrifices.

a 44:19 Or, "in this place of jackals."
b 44:19 Implied in the text.
c 44:20-21 Implied in the context.

[The Future]

23So wake up, Lord God!
Why would you sleep when we're in trouble?
Are you forsaking us forever?
24You can't hide your face any longer from us!
How could you forget our agonizing sorrow?
25Now we lay facedown, sinking into the dust of death,
The quicksand of the grave.
26Arise, awake, and come to help us, O Lord.
Let your unfailing love save us from this sorrow!

Psalm 45

THE WEDDING SONG

For the Pure and Shining One—by the prophetic singers of Korah's clan
A contemplative song of instruction for the Loved One
To the melody of "Lilies"[a]

1My heart is on fire, boiling over with passion.
Bubbling up within me are these beautiful lyrics
As a lovely poem to be sung for the King!
Like a river bursting its banks, I'm overflowing with words,
Spilling out into this sacred story.[b]

[His Royal Majesty]

2You are the most wonderful and winsome of all men.[c]
Elegant grace pours out through every word you speak.[d]
Truly, God has anointed you, his Favored One for eternity!
3Now strap your lightning-sword of judgment upon your side,
O Mighty Warrior, so majestic!
You are full of beauty and splendor as you go out to war!
4In your glory and grandeur go forth in victory!
Through your faithfulness and meekness
The cause of truth and justice will stand.
Awe-inspiring miracles are accomplished by your power,
Leaving everyone dazed and astonished!
5Your wounding leaves men's hearts defeated as they fall before you broken.
6Your glory-kingdom, O God, endures forever,
For you are enthroned to rule with a justice-scepter in your hand!
7You are passionate for righteousness and you hate lawlessness.
This is why God, your God, crowns you with bliss above
Your fellow-kings. He has anointed you, more than any other,

a Lilies in the Bible are metaphors of God's precious people. See Song of Songs 2:1–2, Hosea 14:5, and Luke 12:27–28. Many believe this was the wedding song composed for Solomon as he married the princess of Egypt. But the language is so lofty and glorious that we see One greater than Solomon in its verses. This is a song of the wedding of Jesus and his Bride, the church.
b 45:1 The Hebrew is literally, "my tongue is the pen of a skillful (inspired) scribe."
c 45:2 Or, "Beautiful! Beautiful! Beyond the sons of men!"
d 45:2 See John 6:68 and 7:46.

With his oil of fervent joy, the very fragrance of heaven's gladness.
8Your royal robes release the scent of suffering love for your bride;[a]
The odor of aromatic incense is upon you.[b]
From the pure and shining place, [c]
Such lovely music that makes you glad is played for your pleasure.

[Her Royal Majesty]

9The daughters of kings, women of honor, are maidens in your courts.
And standing beside you, glistening in your pure and golden glory,
Is the beautiful bride-to-be![d]
10Now listen, daughter, pay attention, and forget about your past.
Put behind you every attachment to the familiar,
Even those who once were close to you!
11For your Royal Bridegroom is ravished by your beautiful brightness.
Bow in reverence before him, for he is your Lord!
12Wedding presents pour in from those of great wealth.[e]
The royal friends of the Bridegroom shower you with gifts.
13As the Princess-Bride enters the palace,
How glorious she appears within the holy chamber,
Robed with a wedding dress embroidered with pure gold!
14Lovely and stunning she leads the procession with all her bridesmaids[f]
As they come before you, her Bridegroom-King.
15What a grand, majestic entrance! A joyful, glad procession
As they enter the palace gates!
16Your many sons will one day be kings, just like their Father.
They will sit on royal thrones all around the world.
17I will make sure the fame of your name is honored in every generation
As all the people praise you, giving you thanks forever and ever!

a 45:8 The Hebrew word *myrrh* is taken from a root word that means suffering. Jewish Rabbis refer to myrrh as "tears from a tree," a symbol of suffering love.
b 45:8 The text reads, "aloes and cassia." They both are equated with the anointing spice, the incense burned in the Holy Place.
c 45:8 Or, "from the ivory palaces." This is an obvious reference to the Holy Place, as our High Priest comes from the chamber of glory to be with us. The word *ivory* is taken from a Hebrew word for white and glistening.
d 45:9 Or, "queen."
e 45:12 The Hebrew text is literally "the daughter of Tyre." This was symbolic of the merchants of the earth, those possessing great wealth.
f 45:14 Or, "virgins." See Revelation 14:1–4 and 2 Corinthians 11:2.

Psalm 46

GOD ON OUR SIDE!

For the Pure and Shining One, by the prophetic singers of Korah's clan
A poetic song to the melody of "Hidden Things"[a]

1God, you're such a safe and powerful place to hide!
You're a proven help in time of trouble;
More than enough and always available
Whenever I need you.[b]
2So we will never fear
Even if every structure of support[c] were to crumble away!
We will not fear even
When the earth quakes and shakes,
Moving mountains and casting them into the sea!
3For the raging roar of stormy winds and crashing waves
Cannot erode our faith in you.

Pause in his presence

4God has a constantly flowing river whose sparkling streams
Bring joy and delight to his people!
His river flows right through
The city of God-Most-High,
Into his holy dwelling place.
5God is in the midst of his city,[d]
Secure and never shaken.
At daybreak his help will be seen,
With the appearing of the dawn.
6When the nations are in uproar,
With their tottering kingdoms,
God simply raises his voice
And the earth begins to disintegrate before him!

a As translated in the Septuagint. Other versions read, "for the Maidens." Psalm 46 is known as one of the Songs of Zion. The others are Psalms 48, 76, 84, 87, and 122. These are Psalms which praise Jerusalem as God's dwelling place.
b 46:1 Implied in the text of the Psalm.
c 46:2 Or, "earth itself."
d 46:5 This is a reference to Jerusalem, but today God calls his church a *city* on a hill.

7Here he comes![a]
The Commander!
The mighty Lord of Angel-Armies is on our side!
The God of Jacob fights for us!

Pause in his presence

8–9Everyone look!
Come and see the breathtaking wonders of our God.
For he brings both ruin and revival.[b]
And he's the One who makes conflicts to end
Throughout the earth,
Breaking and burning every weapon of war.
10Surrender your anxiety![c]
Be silent and stop your striving
And you will see that I am God.
I am the God above all the nations,
And I will be exalted throughout the whole earth.
11Here he stands!
The Commander!
The Mighty Lord of Angel-Armies is on our side!
The God of Jacob fights for us!

Pause in his presence

a 46:7 Implied in the context.
b 46:8–9 Implied in the text.
c 46:10 The Septuagint reads, "relax."

Psalm 47

THE KING OF ALL THE EARTH

For the Pure and Shining One
By the prophetic singers of Korah's clan
A poetic song

1 Go ahead and celebrate!
Come on and clap your hands everyone!
Shout to God with the raucous sounds of joy!
2 The Lord God Most High is astonishing,
Awesome beyond words!
He's the formidable and powerful King over all the earth.
3 He's the One who conquered the nations before us
And placed them all under our feet.
4 He's marked out our inheritance ahead of time,
Putting us in the front of the line,
Honoring those he loves.[a]

Pause in his presence

5 God arises with the earsplitting shout of his people!
God takes the throne with the fanfare of trumpets.
6 Sing and celebrate! Sing some more, celebrate some more!
Sing your highest song of praise to our King!
7 For God is the Triumphant King;
The powers of earth are all his.
So sing your celebration songs of highest praise
To the Glorious Enlightened One!
8 Our God reigns over every nation!
He reigns on his holy throne over all.
9 All the nobles and princes,
The loving servants of the God of Abraham,
They all gather to worship.
Every warrior's shield is now lowered,
As surrendered trophies before this King.
He has taken his throne,
High and lofty exalted over all!

a Or, "the pride of Jacob." The Septuagint says: "the beauty of Jacob."

Psalm 48

BEAUTIFUL ZION

A poetic song, for the prophetic singers of Korah's clan

1There are so many reasons to describe God as wonderful!
So many reasons to praise him with unlimited praise![a]
2Zion-City is his home; he lives on his holy mountain.
High and glorious, joy-filled and favored.
Zion-Mountain looms in the farthest reaches of the north,[b]
The city of our incomparable King!
3This is his divine abode, an impenetrable citadel,
For he is known to dwell in the Highest Place.
4–6See how the mighty kings united to come against Zion,
Yet when they saw God manifest in front of their eyes
They were stunned.
Trembling, they all fled away gripped with fear.[c]
Seized with panic, they doubled up in frightful anguish,
Like a woman in the labor pains of childbirth.
7Like a hurricane blowing and breaking the invading ships,[d]
God blows upon them and breaks them to pieces.
8We have heard about these wonders,
And then we saw them with our own eyes.
For this is the city of the Commander of Angel-Armies,
The city of our God, safe and secure forever!

Pause in his presence

9Lord, as we worship you in your temple
We recall over and over
Your kindness to us and your unending love.
10The fame of your name echoes throughout the entire world,
Accompanied with praises!

a 48:1 This Psalm was written to commemorate the defeat of the Assyrian army in the days of King Hezekiah.
b 48:2 Or "the sides of the north," a metaphor to describe God's heavenly home. See also Isaiah 14:13.
c 48:4–6 This no doubt refers to the night the angel of the Lord descended into the ranks of the Assyrians and killed 185,000 men. See Isaiah 37:36.
d 48:7 Or, "ships of Tarshish."

Your right hand is full of victory.
11So let the people of Zion rejoice with gladness;
Let the daughters of praise leap for joy![a]
For God will see to it that you are judged fairly.
12-13Circle Zion; count her towers.
Consider her walls, climb her palaces,
And then go and tell the coming generation
Of the care and compassion of our God.
14Yes, this is our God, our great God forever.
He will lead us onward until the end,
Through all time, beyond death,
And into eternity!

a 48:11 Or, "the daughters of Judah."

Psalm 49

WISDOM BETTER THAN WEALTH

For the Pure and Shining One
A poetic song by the prophetic singers of Korah's clan

1-2 Listen one and all! Both rich and poor together,
All over the world—everyone listen to what I have to say!
3 For wisdom will come from my mouth,
Words of insight and understanding will be heard
From the musings of my heart.
4 I will break open mysteries with my music,
And my song will release riddles solved.
5 There's no reason to fear when troubling times come,
Even when you're surrounded with problems
And persecutors who chase at your heels.[a]
6-7 They trust in their treasures and boast in their riches,
Yet not one of them, though rich as a king,
Could rescue his own brother from the guilt of his sins.
Not one could give God the ransom price
For the soul of another, let alone for himself!
8-9 A soul's redemption is too costly and precious
For anyone to pay with earthly wealth.
The price to pay is never enough
To purchase eternal life for even one,
To keep them out of hell.
10-11 The brightest and best,
Along with the foolish and senseless,
God sees that they all will die one day,
Leaving their houses and wealth to others.
Even though they name streets and lands after themselves,[b]
Hoping to have their memory endure beyond the grave,
Legends in their own minds,

a 49:5 This phrase contains a variant form of the name *Jacob*, which means heel-grabber.
b 49:10–11 Or, "they read their names in the ground."

Their home address is now the cemetery!
12The honor of man is short-lived and fleeting.
There's so little difference between man and beast,
For both will one day perish.
13Such is the path of foolish men,
And those who quote everything they say,
For they are here today and gone tomorrow!

Pause in his presence

14A shepherd called "Death" herds them,
Leading them like mindless sheep straight to hell.
Yet at daybreak you will find the righteous ruling in their place.
Every trace of them will be gone forever,
With all their "glory" lost in the darkness of their doom.
15But I know the loving God will redeem my soul,
Raising me up from the dark power of death,
Taking me as his bridal partner.[a]

Pause in his presence

16So don't be disturbed when you see the rich
Surround you with the "glory" of their wealth on full display.
17For when they die they will carry nothing with them,
And their riches will not follow them beyond the grave.
18–19Though they have the greatest rewards of this world
And all applaud them for their accomplishments,
They will follow those who have gone before them
And go straight into the realm of darkness
Where they never ever see the light again.
20So this is the way of mortal man;
Honored for a moment
Yet without eternal insight,
Like a beast that will one day perish.

a 49:15 Or, "He will offer his hand to me in marriage."

Psalm 50

GOD HAS SPOKEN

A poetic song of Asaph, the gatherer[a]

1The God of gods, the mighty Lord himself, has spoken!
He shouts out over all the people of the earth,
In every brilliant sunrise and every beautiful sunset, saying,
"Listen to me!"[b]
2God's glory-light shines out of the Zion-realm[c]
With the radiance of perfect beauty.
3With the rumble of thunder he approaches;
He comes with an earsplitting sound!
All around him are furious flames of fire,
And preceding him is the dazzling blaze of his glory.
4Here he comes to judge his people!
He summons his court with heaven and earth as his jury, saying:
5"Gather all my lovers,
My godly ones whose hearts are one with me,
Those who have entered into my holy covenant
By sacrifices upon the altar."
6And the heavens respond:
"God himself will be their Judge,
And he will judge them with righteousness!"
Pause in his presence
7Listen to me, O my people! Listen well, for I am your God!
I am bringing you to trial and here are my charges.
8I do not rebuke you for your sacrifices,
Which you continually bring to my altar.
9Do I need your young bull or goats from your fields
As if I was hungry?[d]

a Asaph's name means gatherer. Like David, Asaph was anointed with the Spirit of prophecy and wrote twelve Psalms (Psalms 50 and 73–83).
b 50:1 Implied in the text.
c 50:2 The Aramaic text can be translated, "Out of Zion God has shown a glorious crown."
d 50:9 Implied in the context.

10-11Every animal of field and forest belongs to me, the Creator.
I know every movement of the birds in the sky,
And every animal of the field is in my thoughts.
The entire world and everything it contains is mine.
12-13If I were hungry do you think I would tell you?
For all that I have created, the fullness of the earth is mine.
Am I fed by your sacrifices? Of course not!
14Why don't you bring me the sacrifices I desire?
Bring me your true and sincere thanks, and show your
Gratitude by keeping your promises to me, the Most High.
15Honor me by trusting in me in your day of trouble.
Cry aloud to me, and I will be there to rescue you.
That is what I desire from you![a]
16And now I speak to the wicked. Listen to what I have to say to you!
What right do you have to presume to speak for me
And claim my covenant promises as yours?
17For you have hated my instruction, and disregarded my words,
Throwing them away as worthless!
18You forget to condemn the thief or adulterer.
You are their friend, running alongside them into darkness!
19-20The sins of your mouth multiply evil! You have a lifestyle of lies,
Devoted to deceit as you speak against others,
Even slandering those of your own household!
21All this you have done and I kept silent, so you thought
That I was just like you, sanctioning evil. But now I will bring you
To my courtroom and spell out clearly my charges before you!
22This is your last chance; my final warning! Your time is up!
Turn away from all this evil, or the next time you hear from me
It will be when I am coming to pass sentence upon you.[b]
I will snatch you away and no one will be there
To help you escape my judgment!
23The life that pleases me is a life lived in the gratitude of grace,
Always choosing to walk with me in what is right.
This is the sacrifice I desire from you! If you do this,
More of my salvation will unfold for you!

a 50:15 Implied in the context.
b 50:22 Implied in the context.

Psalm 51

A PRAYER OF REPENTANCE

For the Pure and Shining One
A prayer of confession when the prophet Nathan exposed
King David's adultery with Bathsheba[a]

1-2God, give me grace from your fountain of forgiveness!
I know your abundant love is enough to wash away my guilt.
Take away this shameful guilt of sin.
Forgive the full extent of my wrong,
And erase this deep stain on my conscience.
3-4For I'm so ashamed. I feel such pain and anguish within me,
I can't get away from the sting of my sin against you, Lord!
Everything I did, I did right in front of you, for you saw it all.
Everything you say to me is infallibly true
And your judgment conquers me.
5Lord, I have been a sinner from birth.
Sin's corruption has polluted my soul.
6I know that you delight to set your truth deep in my spirit.
So come into the hidden places of my heart
And teach me wisdom.
7Purify my conscience! Make this leper clean again![b]
Wash me in your love until I am pure in heart.[c]
8Satisfy me in your sweetness, and my song of joy will return.
The places within me you have crushed
Will rejoice in your healing touch.[d]
9Hide my sins from your face;
Erase all my guilt in your saving grace.
10Start over with me, and create a new, clean heart within me.[e]

a This Psalm is based on the incident that is recorded in 2 Samuel 12–13.
b 51:7 The Hebrew text contains the word *hyssop*. This was a bushy plant used for sprinkling blood on a healed leper to ceremonially cleanse him for the worship of God. See Leviticus 14:3–7 and Numbers 19.
c 51:7 Or, "Wash me with the snow from above so I can be whitened."
d 51:9 In this beautiful verse, the "broken places" are literally "broken bones." Our bones speak allegorically of our inner being, our emotional strength.
e 51:10 The word used for *create* takes us back to Genesis 1, and it means to create from nothing. David now knows he had no goodness without God placing it within him.

Fill me with pure thoughts
And holy desires, ready to please you.
11May there never be even a shadow of darkness between us!
May you never deprive me of your Sacred Spirit!
12Let my passion for life be restored,
Tasting joy in every breakthrough you bring to me.
Give me more of your Holy Spirit-Wind[a]
So that I may stand strong and true to you!
13Then I can show to other guilty ones
How loving and merciful you are.
They will find their way back home to you,
Knowing that you will forgive them.
14O God, my saving God,
Deliver me fully from every sin,
Even the sin that brought blood-guilt to my soul.
Then my heart will once again be thrilled to sing
The passionate songs of righteousness and forgiveness!
15Lord God, unlock my heart, unlock my lips,
And I will overcome with my joyous praise!
16For the source of your pleasure is not in my performance
Or the sacrifices I might offer to you.
17The fountain of your pleasure is found
In the sacrifice of my shattered heart before you.
You will not despise my tenderness
As I humbly bow down at your feet!
18Lord, don't punish others for my sin;[b]
Keep showing favor to Zion.
Be the protecting wall around Jerusalem.
19And when we are fully restored[c]
You will rejoice and take delight
In every offering of our lives;
As we bring our every sacrifice of righteousness
Before you in love!

a 51:12 The Hebrew word for *spirit* is also the word for *wind*.
b 51:18 Implied in the text.
c 51:19 Implied in the text.

Psalm 52

THE FATE OF CYNICS

For the Pure and Shining One
A song of instruction by King David composed when Doeg, the Edomite, betrayed David to Saul, saying: "David has come to the house of Ahimilech!"[a]

1You call yourself a mighty man, a big shot?
Then why do you boast in the evil you have done?
Yet God's constant love and mercy will endure and carry the day!
2Listen, O deceiver, trickster of others:
Your words are wicked, harming and hurting all who hear them!
3You love evil and hate what is good and right.
You would rather lie than tell the truth.

Pause in his presence

4You love to distort, confuse, and deceive,
Using your sly tongue to spin the truth.
5But the Almighty will soon strike you down!
He will pull you up by your roots
And drag you away to the darkness of death.

Pause in his presence

6The godly will see all this and will be awestruck.
Then they will laugh at the wicked, saying,
7"See what happens to those great in their own eyes
Who don't trust in God to save them!
Look how they trusted only in their wealth
And made their living from wickedness."
8But I am like a flourishing olive tree, anointed in the house of God.[b]
I trust in the unending love of God;
His passion toward me is forever and ever.
9Because it is finished[c]
I will be praising you forever and giving you thanks!
Before all your godly lovers
I will proclaim your beautiful name!

a For this episode in David's life, see 1 Samuel 21:1–9; 22:9–23.
b 52:8 Implied in the text. The olive tree was the source of the sacred anointing oil.
c 52:9 The words "It is finished" were the last words of Jesus on the cross.

Psalm 53

THE WICKEDNESS OF THE WORLD

For the Pure and Shining One
A contemplative song of instruction to the tune of "The Dance of Mourning"

1Only the withering soul would say to himself,[a]
"There's no God for me!"
Anyone who thinks like that is corrupt and callous;
Depraved and detestable, they are devoid of what is good.
2The Lord looks down in love, bending over heaven's balcony.
God looks over all of Adam's sons and daughters;
Looking to see if there are any who are wise with insight—
Any who search for him, wanting to please him?
3But no, all have wandered astray,
Walking stubbornly toward evil.
Not one is good; he can't even find one!
4Look how they live in luxury while exploiting my people.
Won't these workers of wickedness ever learn!
They never even think of praying to me.
5Soon, unheard-of terror will seize them while in their sins.
God himself will one day scatter the bones
Of those who rose up against you.
Doomed and rejected they will be put to shame,
For God has despised them!
6Oh, I wish our time of rescue were already here,
Oh, that God would come forth now—
Arising from the midst of his Zion-people
To save and restore his very own.
What gladness and joy will break forth
When the Lord has rescued Israel!

a 53:1 The word for *fool* comes from a Hebrew word meaning withering. If we make no room for God, we have a withered heart; and our moral sense of righteousness is put to sleep, and the noble aspirations of the heart shrivel up and die.

Psalm 54

DEFEND ME

For the Pure and Shining One, David's contemplative song of instruction
A song of derision[a] *when the Ziphites betrayed David to Saul, saying:*
"David is hiding among us, come and get him!"

1 God, for your name's sake, defend me with your might!
Come with your glorious power and save me!
2 Listen to my prayer; turn your ears to my cry!
3 These violent men have risen up against me;
Heartless, ruthless men
Who care nothing about God,
They seek to take my life.

Pause in his presence

4 But the Lord God has become my wraparound Shield.
He leans into my heart
And lays his hands upon me![b]
5 God will see to it that
Those who sow evil will reap evil.
So Lord, in your great faithfulness,
Destroy them once and for all!
6 Lord, I will offer myself freely,
And everything I am I give to you.
I will worship and praise your name, O Lord,
For it is precious to me.
7 Through you I'm saved, rescued from every trouble.
I've seen with my eyes the defeat of my enemies.
I've triumphed over them all!

a The Hebrew word used here and translated in some versions as *stringed instrument* can also be rendered *a song of mocking.*
b 54:4 The word used here is *uphold* or *sustain*. It comes from a root word that means to lean upon or to lay hands upon. The translation uses both concepts in this verse.

Psalm 55

BETRAYED

To the Pure and Shining One
King David's song of derision, for instruction

1God, listen to my prayer!
Don't hide your heart from me when I cry out to you!
2-3Come close to me and give me your answer.
Here I am, moaning, and restless.
I'm preoccupied with the threats of my enemies
And crushed by the pressure of their opposition.
They surround me with trouble and terror.
In their fury they rise up against me
In an angry uproar.
4My heart is trembling inside my chest
As the terror of death seizes me.
5Fear and dread overwhelm me.
I shudder before the horror I face.
6I say to myself, "If only I could fly away from all of this!
If only I could run away to the place of rest and peace.
7I would run far away where no one could find me,
Escaping to a wilderness retreat."

Pause in his presence

8I will hurry off to hide in the higher place,
Into my Shelter, safe from this raging storm and tempest.
9God, confuse them until they quarrel with themselves.
Destroy them with their own violent strife and slander!
They have divided the city with their discord.
10Though they patrol the walls night and day against invaders
The real danger is within the city!
It's the misery and strife in the heart of its people.
11Murder is in their midst.
Wherever you turn you find trouble and ruin.
12It wasn't an enemy who taunted me.

If it was my enemy, filled with pride and hatred,
Then I could have endured it. I would have just run away.
13But it was you, my intimate friend, one like a brother to me.
It was you, my advisor,[a] the companion
I walked with and worked with!
14We once had sweet fellowship with each other.
We worshipped in unity as one,
Celebrating together with God's people.[b]
15Now desolation and darkness come upon you.
May you and all those like you descend into the pit of destruction!
Since evil has been your home, may evil now bury you alive!
16But as for me, I will call upon the Lord to save me, and I know he will!
17Every evening I will explain my need to him.
Every morning I will move my soul toward him.
Every waking hour I will worship only him,
And he will hear and respond to my cry.
18Though many wish to fight,
And the tide of battle turns against me,
By your power I will be safe and secure;
Peace will be my portion.
19God himself will hear me!
God-Enthroned through everlasting ages,
The God of Unchanging Faithfulness,
He will put them in their place,
All those who refuse to love and revere him!

Pause in his presence

20 I was betrayed by my friend, though I live in peace with him.
While he was stretching out his hand of friendship
He was secretly breaking every promise he had ever made to me!
21His words were smooth and so charming.
Yet his heart was disloyal, and full of hatred.
His words so soft as silk while all the time scheming my demise.
22So here's what I've learned through it all:
Leave all your cares and anxieties at the feet of the Lord,

a 55:13 The Greek word in the Septuagint can be translated as a seer (prophet).
b 55:14 David is speaking of Ahithophel who had once been his friend and advisor, only to betray him. This is foreshadowing of what happened between Jesus and Judas.

And measureless grace will strengthen you.
23He will watch over his lovers,
Never letting them slip or be overthrown.
He will send all my enemies to the pit of destruction.
Murderers, liars, and betrayers will face an untimely death.
My life's hope and trust is in you, and you'll never fail to rescue me!

Psalm 56

TRUSTING IN GOD

For the Pure and Shining One
King David's golden song of instruction composed when the Philistines captured him in Gath
To the tune "The Oppression of the Princes to Come" [a]

1Lord, show me Your kindness and mercy,
For these men oppose and oppress me all day long.
2Not a day goes by but that somebody harasses me.
So many in their pride
Trample me under their feet.[b]
3But in the day that I'm afraid,
I lay all my fears before you
And trust in you with all my heart.
4What harm could a man bring to me?
With God on my side I will not be afraid of what comes.
The roaring praises of God fill my heart,
And I will always triumph as I trust his promises.
5Day after day cruel critics distort my words;
Constantly they plot my collapse.
6Lurking in the dark, waiting,
Spying on my movements in secret,
To take me by surprise, ready to take my life.
7They don't deserve to get away with this!
Look at their wickedness, their injustice, Lord!
In your fierce anger cast them down to defeat!
8You've kept track of all my wandering and my weeping.
You've stored my many tears in your bottle—not one will be lost.
You care about me every time I've cried.[c]
For it is all recorded in your book of remembrance.[d]
9The very moment I call to you for a Father's help

a Or, "the distant dove of silence."
b 56:2 The Septuagint says, "they war with me in the high places."
c Implied in the text.
d 56:8 See also Malachi 3:16.

The tide of battle turns and my enemies flee!
This one thing I know: God is on my side!
10I trust in the Lord.
And I praise him!
I trust in the Word of God.
And I praise him!
11What harm could man do to me?
With God on my side I will not be afraid of what comes.
My heart overflows with praise to God and for his promises.
I will always trust in him.
12 So I'm thanking you with all my heart,
With gratitude for all you've done.
I will do everything I've promised you, Lord.
13For you have saved my soul from death
And my feet from stumbling
So that I can walk before the Lord
Bathed in his life-giving light.

Psalm 57

TRIUMPHANT FAITH

To the Pure and Shining One
King David's golden song of instruction composed when he hid from Saul in a cave[a]
To the tune "Do Not Destroy"

1Please God, show me mercy!
Open your grace-fountain for me,
For you are my soul's true Shelter.
I will hide beneath the shadow of your embrace,
Under the wings of your cherubim
Until this terrible trouble is past.
2I will cry out to you, the God of the highest heaven,
The mighty God, who performs all these wonders for me.
3From heaven he will send a Father's help to save me.[b]
He will trample down
Those who trample me.

Pause in his presence

For he will always show me love
By his gracious and constant care.
4I am surrounded by these fierce and brutal men.
They are like lions just wanting to tear to me shreds.
Why must I continue to live among these seething terrorists,
Breathing out their angry threats and insults against me?
5Lord God, be exalted as you soar throughout the heavens.
May your shining glory be seen in the skies!
Let it be seen high above over all the earth!
6For they have set a trap[c] for me.
Frantic fear has me overwhelmed.
But look! The very trap they set for me
Has sprung shut upon themselves instead of me!

Pause in his presence

a This incident is recorded in 1 Samuel 24.
b 57:3 Implied in the text.
c 57:6 The Septuagint says, "they have dug a cesspool in front of me."

7My heart, O God, is quiet and confident.
Now I can sing with passion your wonderful praises!
8Awake, O my soul, with the music of his splendor-song!
Arise my soul and sing his praises!
My worship will awaken the dawn,
Greeting the daybreak with my songs of light![a]
9Wherever I go I will thank you, my God.
Among all the nations they will hear
My praise songs to you.
10Your love is so extravagant,
It reaches to the heavens!
Your faithfulness so astonishing,
It stretches to the sky!
11Lord God, be exalted as you soar throughout the heavens.
May your shining glory be shown in the skies!
Let it be seen high above all the earth!

a 57:8 Implied in the text.

Psalm 58

JUDGE OF THE JUDGES

For the Pure and Shining One
King David's golden song of instruction
To the tune "Do Not Destroy"

1-2 God's justice? You high and mighty politicians
Know nothing about it!
Which one of you has walked in justice toward others?
Which one of you has treated everyone right and fair?
Not one!
You only give "justice" in exchange for a bribe.
For the right price you let others get away with murder.
3-4 Wicked wanderers even from the womb! That's who you are!
Lying with your words—your teaching is poison.[a]
5 Like cobras closing their ears to the most expert of the charmers,
You strike out against all who are near.[b]
6 O God, break their fangs;
Shatter the teeth of these ravenous lions!
7 Let them disappear like water falling on thirsty ground.
Let all their weapons be useless.
8 Let them be like snails dissolving into the slime.
Let them be cut off, never seeing the light of day!
9 God will sweep them away so fast
That they'll never know what hit them.[c]
10 The godly will celebrate in the triumph of good over evil.
And the lovers of God will trample
The wickedness of the wicked under their feet!
11 Then everyone will say,
"There is a God who judges the judges";
And "there is a great reward in loving God!"

a 58:3-4 The Hebrew says "venom of a serpent," which is a clear metaphor for wrong teaching.
b 58:5 Implied in the context.
c 58:9 The Hebrew here is recognized by nearly every scholar to be one of the most difficult verses in the Psalms to translate.

Psalm 59

PROTECT ME

For the Pure and Shining One, King David's song of instruction composed when Saul set an ambush for him at his home[a]
To the tune "Do Not Destroy"

1My God, protect me! Keep me safe from all my enemies,
For they're coming to kill me.
Put me in a high place out of their reach,
A place so high that these assassins will never find me.
2Save me from these murdering men,
These bloodthirsty killers.
3See how they set an ambush for my life.
They're fierce men ready to launch their attack against me.
God, I'm innocent, protect me![b]
4I've done nothing to deserve this,
Yet they are already plotting together to kill me.
Arise, Lord, see what they're scheming
And come and meet with me.
5Awaken, O God of Israel!
Commander of Angel-Armies,
Arise to punish
These treacherous people who oppose you!
Don't go soft on these hardcase killers!

Pause in his presence

6After dark they came to spy, sneaking around the city,
Snarling, prowling like a pack of stray dogs in the night;
7Boiling over with rage, shouting out their curses,
Convinced that they'll never get caught.
8But you, Lord, break out laughing at their plans,
Amused by their arrogance, scoffing at their sinful ways.
9My strength is found when I wait upon you.

a This incident is recorded in 1 Samuel 19:11–18.
b 59:3 Implied in the context.

Watch over me, God, for you are my Mountain Fortress;
You set me on high!
10The God of passionate love will meet with me.
My God will empower me
To rise in triumph over my foes.
11Don't just kill them all;
Stagger them with a vivid display of power.
And scatter them with your armies of angels,
O mighty God, our Protector!
Make them as wanderers and vagabonds,
So that when we encounter them no one will forget[a]
How you brought us to victory.
12They are nothing but proud, cursing liars.
They sin in every word they speak,
Boasting in their blasphemies!
13May your wrath be kindled to destroy them—
Finish them off!
Make an end of them and their deeds
Until they are no more!
Let them all know and learn
That God is the Ruler over his people,[b]
The God-King over all the earth!

Pause in his presence

14Here they come again! Prowling, growling
Like a pack of stray dogs in the city
15Drifting, devouring, and coming in for the kill.[c]
16But as for me, your strength shall be my song of joy.
At each and every sunrise
My lyrics of your love will fill the air!
For you have been my Glory-Fortress,
A Stronghold in my day of distress.
17O my Strength, I sing with joy your praises.
O my Stronghold, I sing with joy your song!
O my Savior, I sing with joy the lyrics
Of your faithful love for me!

a 59:11 Implied in the text.
b 59:13 The Hebrew is literally "God of Jacob."
c 59:15 Implied in the context.

Psalm 60

HAS GOD FORGOTTEN US?

To the Pure and Shining One
King David's poem for instruction composed when he fought against the Syrians with the outcome still uncertain and Joab turned back to kill 12,000 descendants of Esau in the Valley of Salt
To the tune of "Lily of the Covenant"

1God, it seemed like you walked off and left us!
Why have you turned against us? Have you deserted us?
O Lord, we plead, come back and help us as a Father.[a]
2The earth quivers and quakes before you,
Splitting open and breaking apart.
Now come and heal it,[b] for it is shaken to its depths.
3You have taught us hard lessons
And made us drink the wine of bewilderment.
4You have given miraculous signs to those who love you.
As we follow you we fly the flag of truth,
And all who love the truth will rally to it.

Pause in his presence

5Come to your beloved ones and gently draw us out!
Answer our prayer for your saving help.
Come with your might and strength,
For we need you, Lord![c]
6-7Then I heard the Lord speak in his holy splendor,
From his sanctuary I heard the Lord promise:
"In my triumph I will be the One
To measure out the portion of my inheritance to my people,
And I will secure the land as I promised you.
Shechem, Succoth, Gilead, Manasseh;
They are all still mine!" he says.
"Judah will continue to produce kings and lawgivers;

a 60:1 Implied in the context.
b 60:2 Implied in the text.
c 60:5 Implied in the text.

And Ephraim will produce great warriors.
8Moab will become my lowly servant!
Edom will likewise serve my purposes!
I will lift up a shout of victory over the land of Philistia!
9But who will bring my triumph into the strong city,
Into Edom's fortresses?"[a]
10Have you really rejected us, refusing to fight our battles?
11Give us a Father's help when we face our enemies.
For to trust in any man is an empty hope.
12With God's help we will fight like heroes,
And trample down our every foe!

a 60:9 *Edom* is a variant form of the word *Adam*.

Psalm 61

PRAYER FOR PROTECTION

To the Pure and Shining One
A song for the guitar by King David

1O God, hear my prayer. Listen to my heart's cry.
2For no matter where I am, even when I'm far from home
I will cry out to you for a Father's help.
When I'm feeble and overwhelmed by life,
Guide me into your glory where I am safe and sheltered.
3Lord, you are a paradise of protection to me.
You lift me high above the fray.
None of my foes can touch me,
When I'm held firmly in your wraparound presence!
4Keep me in this glory.
Let me live continually under your splendor-shadow;
Hiding my life in you forever.

Pause in his presence

5You have heard my sweet resolutions
To love and serve you, for I am your beloved.
And you have given me
An inheritance of rich treasures
Which you give to all your lovers.
6You treat me like a king,
Giving me a full and abundant life,
Years and years of reigning,[a]
Like many generations rolled into one.
7I will live enthroned with you forever!
Guard me, God, with your unending, unfailing love.
Let me live my days walking in grace and truth before you.
8And my praises will fill the heavens forever,
Fulfilling my vow to make every day a love gift to you!

a 61:6 Or, "add to the days of the king."

Psalm 62

UNSHAKABLE FAITH

To the Pure and Shining One
King David's melody of love's celebration[a]

1I stand silently to listen for the One I love,
Waiting as long as it takes for the Lord to rescue me.
For God alone has become my Savior.
2He alone is my Safe Place;
His wrap-around presence always protects me.
For he is my Champion Defender;
There's no risk of failure with God.
So why would I let worry paralyze me,
Even when troubles multiply around me?
3But look at these who want me dead,
Shouting their vicious threats at me!
The moment they discover my weakness
They all begin plotting to take me down.
4Liars, hypocrites,
With nothing good to say.
All of their energies are spent
On moving me from this exalted place.

Pause in his presence

5I am standing in absolute stillness,
Silent before the One I love;
Waiting as long as it takes for him to rescue me.
Only God is my Savior, and he will not fail me.
6For he alone is my Safe Place,
His wrap-around presence always protects me,
As my Champion Defender;
There's no risk of failure with God!
So why would I let worry paralyze me,

a The inscription includes the name *Jeduthun*, which means one who praises.

Even when troubles multiply around me?
[7]God's glory is all around me!
His wrap-around presence is all I need,
For the Lord is my Savior,
My Hero, and my life-giving strength.
[8]Join me, everyone! Trust only in God every moment!
Tell him all your troubles and
Pour out your heart-longings to him.
Believe me when I tell you—he will help you!

Pause in his presence

[9]Before God, all the people of the earth, high or low,
Are like smoke that disappears,
Like a vapor that quickly vanishes away.
Compared to God they're nothing but vanity, nothing at all!
[10]The wealth of the world is nothing to God.
So if your wealth increases, don't be boastful or
Put your trust in your money.
And don't you think for a moment that
You can get away with stealing
By overcharging others,
Just to get more for yourself!
[11]God said to me once and for all,
"All the strength and power you need flows from me!"
And again I heard it clearly said,
[12]"All the love you need is found in me!"
And the Almighty said,
"The greater your passion for more—
The greater reward I will give you!"[a]

a 62:12 Implied in the text.

Psalm 63

THIRSTING FOR GOD

For the Pure and Shining One
King David's song when he was exiled in the Judean wilderness

1O God of my life,
I'm lovesick for you in this weary wilderness.
I thirst with the deepest longings to love you more,
With cravings in my heart that can't be described.
Such yearning grips my soul for you, my God!
2I'm energized every time I enter
Your heavenly sanctuary to seek more of your power
And drink in more of your glory.
3For your tender mercies
Mean more to me than life itself.
How I love and praise you, God!
4Daily I will worship you
Passionately and with all my heart.
My arms will wave to you like banners of praise.
5 I overflow with praise when I come before you,
For the anointing of your presence
Satisfies me like nothing else.
You are such a rich banquet of pleasure to my soul.
6-7I lie awake each night thinking of you
And reflecting on how you help me like a Father.
I sing through the night under your splendor-shadow,
Offering up to you my songs of delight and joy!
8With passion I pursue and cling to you.
Because I feel your grip on my life,
I keep my soul close to your heart.
9Those who plot to destroy me
Shall descend into the darkness of hell.

10They will be consumed by their own evil,
And become nothing more than dust under our feet.[a]
11These liars will be silenced forever!
But with the anointing of a king I will dance and rejoice,
Along with all his lovers who trust in him.

a 63:10 Or, "food for foxes."

Psalm 64

THE DESTROYER DESTROYED

For the Pure and Shining One
King David's song

1Lord, can't you hear my cry, my bitter complaint?
Keep me safe from this band of criminals and
2From the conspiracy of these wicked men.
They gather in their secret counsel to destroy me.
3-4Can't you hear their slander, their lies?
Their words are like poison-tipped arrows
Shot from the shadows. They are
Unafraid and have no fear of consequences.
5They set their traps against us in secret;
They strengthen each other, saying,
"No one can see us. Who can stop us?"
They're nothing more than unruly mobs
Joined in their unholy alliance!
6Searching out new opportunities to pervert justice,
Deceivers scheming together their ill-conceived plot
As they plan the "perfect crime."
How unsearchable is their endless evil,
Trying desperately to hide the deep darkness of their hearts.
7But all the while God has his own fire-tipped arrows!
Suddenly, without warning,
They will be pierced and struck down!
8Staggering backward they will be destroyed
By the very ones they spoke against!
All who see this will view them with scorn!
9Then all will stand awestruck over what God has done,
Seeing how he vindicated the victims of these crimes.
10The lovers of God will be glad, rejoicing in the Lord.
They will be found in his glorious wrap-around presence,
Singing songs of praise to God!

Psalm 65

WHAT A SAVIOR

For the Pure and Shining One
King David's poetic song

1-2O God in Zion, to you even silence is praise!
You are the God who answers prayer;[a]
All of humanity comes before you with their requests.
3Though we are overcome by our many sins,
Your sacrifice covers over them all.
4And your priestly lovers, those you've chosen,
Will be greatly favored to be brought close to you.
What inexpressible joys are theirs!
What feasts of mercy fill them in your heavenly sanctuary!
How satisfied we will be just to be near you!
5 You answer our prayers with amazing wonders,
And with awe-inspiring displays of power.
You are the righteous God,
Who helps us like a Father.
Everyone everywhere looks to you,
For you are the Confidence of all the earth,
Even to the farthest islands of the sea.
6What jaw-dropping, astounding power is yours!
You are the Mountain-Maker, who sets them all in place.
7You muzzle the roar of the mighty seas,
And the rage of mobs with their noisy riots.
8O God, to the farthest corners of the planet
People will stand in awe, startled and stunned
By your signs and wonders.
Sunrise brilliance and sunset beauty
Both take turns singing their songs of joy to you.
9Your visitations of glory bless the earth;[b]

a The Aramaic could be translated "to you a vow is paid."
b 65:9 The Septuagint says, "You've made the earth drunk with your visitations."

The rivers of God overflow and enrich it.
You paint the wheat fields golden
As you provide rich harvests.
10 Every field is watered with the abundance of rain,
Showers soaking the earth and softening its clods,
Causing seeds to sprout throughout the land.
11 You crown the earth with its yearly harvest,
The fruits of your goodness.
Wherever you go the tracks of your chariot wheels
Drip with oil.
12 Luxuriant green pastures boast of your bounty
As you make every hillside blossom with joy.
13 The grazing meadows are covered with flocks,
And the fertile valleys are clothed with grain.
Each one dancing and shouting for joy,
Creation's celebration!
And they're all singing their songs of praise to you!

Psalm 66

THANK YOU, LORD

For the Pure and Shining One
A song of awakening[a]

1Everyone everywhere, lift up your joyful shout to God!
2Sing your songs tuned to his glory!
Tell the world how wonderful he is.
3For he's the awe-inspiring God,
Great and glorious in power!
We've never seen anything like him![b]
Mighty in miracles,
You cause your enemies to tremble.
No wonder they all surrender and bow before you!
4All the earth will bow down to worship;
All the earth will sing your glories forever!

Pause in his presence

5Everyone will say: "Come and see
The incredible things God has done;
It will take your breath away!
He multiplies miracles for his people!"[c]
6He made a highway going right through the Red Sea,
As the Hebrews each passed through on dry ground,
Exploding with joyous excitement
Over the miracles of God.
7In his great and mighty power he rules forever,
Watching over every movement of every nation.
So beware, rebel lands; he knows how to humble you!

Pause in his presence

8Praise God, all you peoples.
Praise him everywhere

a As translated from the inscription found in the Septuagint.
b 66:3 Implied in the context.
c 66:5 The Septuagint says, "His works are more to be feared than the decisions of men."

And let everyone know you love him!
9There's no doubt about it;
God holds our lives safely in his hands.
He's the One who keeps us faithfully following him.
10O Lord, we have passed through your fire;
Like precious metal made pure,
You've proved us, perfected us, and made us holy.
11You've captured us, ensnared us in your net.
Then, like prisoners, you placed chains around our necks.[a]
12You've allowed our enemies to prevail against us.
We've passed through fire and flood,
Yet in the end you always bring us out
Better than we were before,
Saturated with your goodness.[b]
13I come before your presence with my sacrifice.
I'll give you all that I've promised, everything I have.
14 When I was overcome in my anguish
I promised to give you my sacrifice—
Here it is! All that I said I would offer you is yours!
15The best I have to bring,
I'll throw it all into the fire
As the fragrance of my sacrifice ascends unto you.[c]

Pause in his presence

16All you lovers of God who want to please him,
Come and listen, and I'll tell you what he did for me.
17I cried aloud to him with all my heart and he answered me!
Now my mouth overflows with the highest praise.
18Yet if I had closed my eyes to my sin
The Lord God would have closed his ears to my prayer.
19But praises rise to God, for he paid attention to my prayer
And answered my cry to him!
20I will forever praise this God
Who didn't close his heart when I prayed
And never said "No" when I asked him for help.
He never once refused to show me his tender love.

a 66:11 Implied in the text.
b 66:12 Or, "You brought us out into a wide-open space [a place of rest]."
c 66:15 The literal Hebrew describes the sacrifice as "burnt offerings of fat beasts and the smoke of rams, bulls, and male goats."

Psalm 67

IT'S TIME TO PRAISE HIM

For the Pure and Shining One
A poetic song of praise for guitar

1God, keep us near your grace-fountain
And bless us!
And when you look down on us,
May your face beam with joy!

Pause in his presence

2Send us out all over the world
So that everyone everywhere
Will discover your ways
And know who you are
And see your power to save!
3Let all the nations burst forth with praise;
Let everyone everywhere love and enjoy you!
4Then how glad the nations will be
When you are their King.
They will sing, they will shout,
For you give true justice to the people.
Yes! You, Lord, are the Shepherd of the nations!

Pause in his presence

5No wonder the peoples praise you!
Let all the people praise you more![a]
6The harvest of the earth is here!
God, the very God we worship
Keeps us satisfied at his banquet of blessings,
7And the blessings keep coming!
Then all the ends of the earth will give him
The honor he deserves
And be in awe of him!

a 67:5 The Septuagint says, "Let all the people come to know you."

Psalm 68

A SONG OF TRIUMPH

For the Pure and Shining One
David's poetic song of praise

1God! Arise with awesome power,
And every one of your enemies will scatter in fear!
2Chase them away, all these God-haters.
Blow them away as a puff of smoke.
Melt them away like wax in the fire.
One good look at you and the wicked vanish.
3But let all your godly-lovers be glad!
Yes, let them all rejoice in your presence
And be carried away with gladness.[a]
Let them laugh and be radiant with joy!
4Let them sing their celebration-songs
For the coming of the Cloud-Rider,
Whose name is Yah! [b]
5-6To the fatherless he is a Father,
To the widow he is a Champion Friend.
To the lonely, he gives a family.
To the prisoner,[c] he leads into prosperity
Until they each sing for joy.
This is our Holy God in his Holy Place!
But for the rebels there is heartache and despair.[d]
7O Lord, it was you who marched in front of your people
Leading them through the wasteland.

Pause in his presence

8The earth shook beneath your feet;
The heavens filled with clouds

a 68:3 As translated from the Septuagint. The Aramaic is: "They rejoice in his sweetness."
b 68:4 More than an abbreviation, the name *Yah* is associated with the God of heaven, the God of highest glory and power.
c 68:5-6 The Septuagint says "the bitter ones."
d 68:6 The Aramaic says "the rebels will dwell among the tombs."

Before the presence of the God of Sinai!
The sacred mountain shook at the sight of
The face of Israel's God!
9You sent the reviving rain upon the weary land,
Showers of blessing to refresh it.
10So there your people settled.
And in your kindness you provided the poor with abundance.
11God Almighty declares the Word of the gospel with power,[a]
And the warring women of Zion deliver its message:[b]
12"The conquering legions
Have themselves been conquered.
Look at them flee!"
Now Zion's women are left to gather the spoils.
13When you sleep between sharpened stakes[c]
I see you sparkling like silver and glistening like gold,
Covered by the beautiful wings of a dove![d]
14When the Almighty found a king for himself
It became white as snow in his shade.[e]
15O huge, magnificent mountain,
You are the mighty Kingdom of God![f]
All the other peaks, though impressive and imposing,
16Look with envy on you, Mount Zion!
For Zion is the mountain
Where God has chosen to live forever.
17Look! The mighty chariots of God!
Ten thousands upon ten thousands,
More than anyone could ever number.
God is at the front,
Leading them all from Mount Sinai into his sanctuary,
With the radiance of holiness upon him.[g]

a 68:11 As translated from the Aramaic.
b 68:11 As translated from the Masoretic text.
c 68:13 The Aramaic word *shaphya* can be translated "sharpened stakes or thorns": an obvious prophecy of the cross and our union with Christ as he was crucified.
d 68:13 As translated from the Aramaic text, this verse contains prophetic hints of Calvary, where Jesus *slept* the sleep of death between the *sharpened stakes* of the cross. The word *you* is plural and points us to our co-crucifixion with Christ.
e 68:14 Every scholar consulted concludes that this verse is difficult, if not impossible to interpret properly and translate accurately. The last words are literally: "snow fell in Zalmon." *Zalmon* (or *Salmon*) was a wooded area and means "shady."
f 68:15 The Septuagint reads "mountain of provision."
g 68:17 The Septuagint says "the Lord sends his provisions from his Holy Place on Mount Sinai."

18He ascends into the heavenly heights
Taking his many captured ones with him,
Leading them in triumphal procession.
And gifts were given to men, even the once rebellious,
So that they may dwell with Yah.
19What a glorious God![a]
He gives us salvation over and over,[b]
Then daily he carries our burdens!

Pause in his presence

20Our God is a mighty God who saves us over and over!
For the Lord, Yahweh, rescues us
From the ways of death many times.
21But he will crush every enemy, shattering their strength.
He will make heads roll,
For they refuse to repent of their stubborn, sinful ways.
22I hear the Lord God saying to all the enemies of his people:
"You'd better come out of your hiding places,
All of you that are doing your best to stay far away from me;[c]
Don't you know there's no place to hide!
23For my people will be the conquerors;
They will soon have you under their feet!
They will crush you until there is nothing left!"[d]
24O God, my King, your triumphal processions
Keep moving onward in holiness;
You're moving onward toward the Holy Place!
25Leaders in front,[e] then musicians,
With young maidens in between striking their tambourines!
26And they sing "Let all God's princely people rejoice!
Let all the congregations bring their blessing to God, saying:
'The Lord of the Fountain! The Lord of the Fountain of life!
The Lord of the Fountain of Israel!'"

a 68:19 The Aramaic is *Maryah*, the Aramaic form of YHWH or Lord Jehovah.
b 68:19 Salvation is in the plural form in the text (*salvations*).
c 68:22 The Hebrew text makes reference to Bashan (a high mountain) and to the depths of the sea. In other words, there's no place to hide.
d 68:23 The Hebrew text is literally: "Your enemies will be food for the dogs."
e 68:25 As translated from the Septuagint. The Hebrew is "singers in front."

27 Astonishingly, it's the favored youth leading the way.[a]
Princes of praise in their royal robes,
And exalted princes are among them,
Along with princes who have wrestled with God.
28-29 Display your strength, God, and we'll be strong!
For your miracles have made us who we are.
Lord, do it again, and parade from your temple your mighty power.
By your command even kings will bring gifts to you.
30 God, rebuke the beast-life that hides within us![b]
Rebuke those who claim to be "strong ones"[c]
That lurk within the congregation
And abuse the people out of their love for money.
So God scatters the people who are spoiling for a fight.
31 Africa will send her noble envoys to you, O God.
They will come running, stretching out their hands in love to you.
32 Let all the nations of the earth sing songs of praise to Almighty God!
Go ahead all you nations—sing your praise to the Lord!

Pause in his presence

33 Make music for the One who strides the ancient skies.
Listen to his thunderous voice of might split open the heavens.
34 Give it up for God, for he alone has all the strength and power!
Proclaim his majesty! For his glory shines down on Israel.
His mighty strength soars in the clouds of glory.
35 God, we are consumed with awe, trembling before you
As your glory streams from your Holy Place.
The God of power shares his mighty strength with Israel
And with all his people.
God, we give our highest praise to you!

a 68:27 The Hebrew includes the names of four sons of Jacob, representing four tribes. Benjamin, the youngest son, means "son of my right hand," or "the favored one." Judah means "praise." Zebulon's name is the word for "exalted." Naphtali means "obtained by wrestling." Each name speaks of a princely group, and is used here poetically not only for Israel but for all of God's "princely people" in this holy procession of worship.

b 68:30 Literal Hebrew: "Rebuke the beasts in the reeds."

c 68:30 This verse has puzzled scholars, and many conclude that the Hebrew text is nearly incomprehensible with tremendous variations in the translation.

Psalm 69

A CRY OF DISTRESS[a]

To the Pure and Shining One
David's poetic song of praise to the tune "Lilies"

1-2God, my God, come and save me!
These floods of trouble have risen higher and higher.
The water is up to my neck!
I'm sinking into the mud with no place to stand,
And I'm about to drown in this storm.
3I'm weary, exhausted with weeping.
My throat is dry, my voice is gone,
My eyes are swollen with sorrow,
And I'm waiting for you, God, to come through for me.
4I can't even count all those who hate me for no reason.
Many influential men want me silenced,
Yet I've done nothing against them.
Must I restore what I never took away?
5God, my life is an open book to you.
You know every sin I've ever done.
For nothing within me is hidden from your sight!
6Lord Yahweh of Angel-Armies,
Keep me from ever being a stumbling block to others,
To those who love you.
Lord God of Israel, don't let what happens to me
Be the source of confusion
To those who are passionate for you.
7Because of my love for you, Lord,
I have been mocked, cursed, and disgraced.
8Even my own brothers, those of my family,
Act as though they don't want anything to do with me.
9My love for you has my heart on fire!

a Psalm 69 is considered one of the most outstanding messianic Psalms, with obvious prophetic references to the sufferings and cross of Jesus Christ. Next to Psalm 22 it is the Psalm most often quoted in the New Testament.

My passion consumes me for your house!
Nothing will turn me away; even though people
Hate me and insult me for loving you,
I know they hate you even more.
10When they see me seeking for more of you
With weeping and fasting,
They all just scoff and scorn at my passion.
11When I humble myself with sorrow over my sin
It gives them a reason to mock me even more.
12The leaders, the influential ones—
How they scorn my passion for you!
I've become the talk of the town;
The theme of drunkards' songs.
13But I keep calling out to you, Lord!
I know you will bend down to listen to me,
For now is the season of favor.
Because of your great love for me,
Your answer to my prayer will be my sure salvation.
14Pull me out of this mess! Don't let me sink!
Rescue me from those who hate me
And from all this trouble I'm in!
15Don't let this flood drown me.
Save me from these deep waters,
Or I'll go down to the pit of destruction.
16-17Oh, Lord God, answer my prayers!
I need to see your tender kindness, your grace,
Your compassion, and your constant love.
Just let me see your face, and turn your heart toward me.
Come running quickly to your servant.
In this deep distress, come and answer my prayer.
18Come closer as a friend and redeem me.
Set me free so my enemies cannot say
That you are powerless.
19See how they dishonor me in shame and disgrace?
You know, Lord, what I'm going through, and you see it all.
20I'm heartsick and heartbroken by it all.
Their contempt has crushed my soul.

I looked for sympathy and compassion
But found only empty stares.
21 I was hungry and they gave me bitter food.
I was thirsty and they offered me vinegar.[a]
22 Let their "feasts" turn to ashes!
Let their "peace and security" become their downfall!
23 Make them blind as bats, groping in the dark!
Let them be feeble, trembling continually!
24-25 Pour out your fury on them all!
Consume them with the fire of your anger!
Burn down the walled palace where they live!
Leave them homeless and desolate!
26 For they come against the one you yourself have struck,
And they scorn the pain of those you've pierced.
27 Pile on them the guilt of their sins!
Don't let them ever go free!
28 Leave them out of your list of the living!
Blot them out of your book of life!
Never name them as your own!
29 I am burdened and broken by this pain.
When your miracle rescue comes to me
It will lift me to the highest place.
30 Then my song will be a burst of praise to you.
My glory-shouts will make your fame even more glorious
To all who hear my praises!
31 For I know, Lord, that my praises mean more to you
Than all my gifts and sacrifices.
32 All your gentle lovers will see God do this for them,[b]
And they'll overflow with gladness.
Let this revive your hearts, all you lovers of God!
33 For God does listen to the poor and needy
And will not abandon his prisoners of love.[c]
34 Let all the universe praise him!
The high heavens and everyone on earth praise him!

a 69:21 This was fulfilled with Jesus being offered vinegar on the cross. See Luke 23:36.
b 69:32 Implied in the text.
c 69:33 Or, "those wearing shackles."

Let the oceans deep with everything in them, keep it up!
35God will come to save his Zion-people.
God will build up his cities of Judah,
For there his people will live in peace.
36All their children will inherit the land,
And the lovers of his name
Will live there safe and secure!

Psalm 70

A CRY FOR HELP

To the Pure and Shining One
David's poetic lament to always remember

1Please Lord! Come quickly and rescue me!
God, show me your favor and restore me.
2Let all who seek my life be humiliated, confused, and ashamed.
God, send them sprawling,
All who wish me evil; they just want me dead.
3Scoff at every scoffer and cause them all to be utter failures!
Let them be ashamed and horrified
Over their complete defeat.
4But let all who passionately seek you
Erupt with excitement and joy
Over what you've done!
Let all your lovers,
Who continually rejoice in the Savior,[a]
Say aloud: "How great and glorious is our God!"
5Lord, in my place of weakness and need,
Won't you turn your heart toward me
And hurry to help me?
For you are my Savior
And I'm always in your thoughts.
So don't delay to deliver me now.
For you are my God.

a 70:4 This verse contains the Hebrew root word for *Yeshua*.

Psalm 71

THE PSALM OF OLD AGE

1Lord, you are my secure shelter. Don't ever let me down!
2Let your justice be my breakthrough.
Bend low to my whispered cry
And save me from all my enemies!
3You're the only place of protection for me.
I keep coming back to hide myself in you,
For you are like a mountain-cliff-fortress where I'm kept safe.
4Let me escape from these cruel and wicked men.
And save me from the evil hands of the evil one.
5For you are my only hope, Lord!
I've hung onto you, trusting in you all my life.
6-7It was you who supported me from the day I was born,
Loving me, helping me through my life's journey.
You've made me into a miracle;
No wonder I trust you and praise you forever!
Many marvel at my success, but I know
It is all because of you, my mighty Protector!
8I'm overflowing with your praise for all you've done,
And your splendor thrills me all day long.
9Now that I'm old, don't set me aside.
Don't let go of me when my strength is spent.
10-11For all my enemies whisper behind my back.
They're waiting for me to fall so they can finish me off.
They're convinced you've left me,
And that you'll never come to my rescue.
They're saying, "Let's get him now! He has no Savior!"
12O God, stay close to me!
Don't just watch from a distance! Hurry to help me, my God!
13Cover these accusers of mine with shame and failure!
Destroy them all, for they only want to kill me!
14No matter what, I'll trust in you to help me.

Nothing will stop me from praising you to magnify your glory!
15I couldn't begin to count the times you've been there for me.
With the skill of a poet I'll never run out of things to say
Of how you faithfully kept me from danger.[a]
16I will come forth in your mighty strength, O my Lord God.[b]
I'll tell everyone that you alone are the Perfect One.
17From my childhood you've been my teacher,
And I'm still telling everyone of your miracle-wonders!
18God, now that I'm old and gray, don't walk away.
Give me grace to demonstrate to the next generation
All your mighty miracles,
And your excitement to show them your magnificent power!
19For your glorious righteousness
Reaches up to the high heavens.
No one could ever be compared to you!
Who is your equal, O God of marvels and wonders?
20Even though you've let us
Sink down with trials and troubles,
I know you will revive us again,
Lifting us up from the dust of death.
21Give us even more greatness than before.
Turn and comfort us once again.
22My loving God, the harp in my heart will praise you.
Your faithful heart toward us will be the theme of my song.
Melodies and music will rise to you, the Holy One of Israel.
23I will shout and sing your praises for all you are to me—
Savior, lover of my soul!
24I'll never stop telling others how perfect you are,
While all those who seek my harm
Slink away ashamed and defeated!

a 71:15 Implied in the text.
b 71:16 Or, "I will enter into the manliness of Lord Jehovah."

Psalm 72

THE RIGHTEOUS KING

Solomon's Psalm [a]

1O God, make the king a godly judge like you
And give the king's son the gift of justice too.
2Help him to give true justice to your people,
Honorably and equally to all.
3Then the mountains of influence will be fruitful,
And from your righteousness
Prosperity and peace flow to all the people.
4May the poor and humble
Have an advocate with the king.
May he consider the children of the poor
And crush the cruel oppressor.
5The sun and moon will stop shining
Before your lovers will stop worshipping;
For ages upon ages the people
Will love and adore you!
6Your favor will fall like rain
Upon our surrendered lives.[b]
Like showers reviving the earth!
7In the days of his reign the righteous will spring forth
With the abundance of peace and prosperity forevermore.
8May he subdue and take dominion from sea to sea;
May he rule from the river to the rim.
9Desert-nomads are bowing at his feet!
Every enemy falling facedown, biting the dust!
10Distant kings will surrender and come with their gifts
From every continent and coastland;
They will offer their tribute to you.[c]

a The Septuagint indicates this could be a Psalm written by David for his son, Solomon. This royal Psalm is a prayer for the king. Read through it as though it is referring to King Jesus—One who is greater than Solomon.
b 72:6 Or, "like rain on mown grass."
c 72:10 Included in the Hebrew text are: kings of Tarshish (Spain), and kings of Sheba and Seba (Ethiopia).

11O King of kings, they will all bow before you.
O King of kings, every nation will one day serve you.
12-13He will care for the needy and neglected
When they cry to him for help.
The humble and helpless will know his kindness,
For with a father's compassion he will save their souls.
14They will be rescued from tyranny and torture,
For their lifeblood is precious in his eyes.
15Long live this King!
May the wealth of the world be laid before him.[a]
May there be ceaseless praise and prayer to him.
May all the blessing be brought to him.
16Bless us with a bountiful harvest,
With golden grain swaying on the mountain fields!
May the cities be full of praising people, fruitful and filled—
17So that his name may be honored forever!
May the fame of his name spring forth!
May it shine on, like the sunshine!
In him all will be blessed to bless others,
And may all the people bless the One who blessed them.
18Praise forever Jehovah God, the God of Israel!
He is the one and only God of wonders,
Surpassing every expectation.
19The blazing glory of his name will be praised forever!
May all the earth overflow with his glory!
Faithful is our King! Amen!
20This concludes the poetry sung by David, Jesse's son.

a 72:14 Or, "the gold of Sheba."

BOOK III

The "Leviticus" Psalms

PSALMS OF WORSHIP AND GOD'S HOUSE

Psalm 73

GOD'S JUSTICE

Asaph's Psalm

[1]No one can deny it—God is really good to Israel,
And to all those with pure hearts.
But I nearly missed seeing it for myself.[a]
[2]Here's my story: I came so close to missing the way.
[3]I was stumbling over what I saw with the wicked.
For when I saw the boasters with such wealth and prosperity
I became jealous over their smug security.
[4-5]Indulging in whatever they wanted, going where they wanted,
Doing what they wanted, and with no care in the world.
No pain, no problems, they seemed to have it made.
They lived as though life would never end.
[6]They didn't even try to hide their pride and opulence.
Cruelty and violence is part of their lifestyle.
[7] Pampered and pompous, vice oozes from their souls;
They overflow with vanity!
[8]They're such snobs—looking down their noses
They even scoff at God!
They are nothing but bullies threatening God's people!
[9]Loudmouths with no fear of God, pretending to know it all!
Windbags full of hot air, impressing only themselves!
[10]Yet the people keep coming back
To listen to more of their same nonsense.
[11]They tell their cohorts, "God will never know.
See, he has no clue of what we're doing."
[12]These are the wicked ones I'm talking about!
They never have to lift a finger,
Living a life of ease while their riches multiply.
[13]Have I been foolish to play by the rules and keep my life pure?
[14]Here I am suffering under your discipline day after day

a 73:1 Implied in the context.

While they sail through life without a care.[a]
15If I had given in to my pain and spoken of what I was really feeling,
It would have sounded like unfaithfulness to the next generation.
16So when I tried to understand it all, I just couldn't.
It was too puzzling—too much of a riddle to me.
17But then, one day I was brought into the sanctuaries of God,
And in the light of glory, my distorted perspective vanished.
The end of the wicked was near![b]
18They're the ones who are on the slippery path,
And God will suddenly let them slide off into destruction,
To be consumed with terrors forever!
19It will be an instant end to all their life of ease;
A blink of the eye and they're swept away by sudden calamity!
They're all nothing more than momentary monarchs,
20Soon to disappear like a dream when one awakes.
So when the rooster crows,
Lord God, you'll despise their life of fantasies.[c]
21When I saw all of this, what turmoil filled my heart;
Piercing my opinions with your truth.
22I was so stupid. I was senseless and ignorant,
Acting like a brute beast before you, Lord.
23Yet, in spite of all this, you comfort me by your counsel;
You draw me closer to you.
24You lead me with your secret wisdom.
And following you brings me into your brightness and glory!
25Whom have I in heaven but you! You're all I want!
No one on earth means as much to me as you.
26Lord, so many times I fail; I fall into disgrace,
But when I trust in you I have a strong and glorious presence
Protecting and anointing me. Forever you're all I need!
27Those who abandon the worship of God will perish.
The false and unfaithful will be silenced, never heard from again.
28But I'll keep coming closer and closer to you, Lord Yahweh,
For your name is good to me. I'll keep telling the world of
Your awesome works, my faithful and glorious God!

a 73:14 Implied in the context.
b 73:17 Implied in the text.
c 73:20 Or, "shadows."

Psalm 74

WE NEED YOU NOW

Asaph's poem of instruction

1Are you really going to leave us, God?
Would you turn your back on us, rejecting your people?
We are yours, your very own.[a]
Will your anger smolder against us forever?
2Don't forget that we are your beloved ones.
Wrap us back into your heart again, for you chose us.
You brought us out of our slavery and bondage,
And made us your favored ones, your Zion-people,
Your home on earth.
3Turn your steps toward this devastation,
Come running to bring your restoring grace to these ruins;[b]
To what the enemy has done to devastate your Holy Place.
4They have come into the very midst of your dwelling place
Roaring like beasts, setting up their banners
To flaunt their conquest!
5Now everything is in shambles!
They've totally destroyed it;
Like a forest chopped down to the ground,
There's nothing's left!
6All of the beauty of the craftsmanship
Of the inner place has been ruined,
Smashed, broken, and shattered![c]
7They've burned it all to the ground!
They've violated your sanctuary,
The very dwelling place of your glory and your name.
8They boasted, "Let's completely crush them!

a 74:1 Or, "the sheep of your pasture."
b 74:3 This verse reads so differently in the Aramaic: "Lift up your servants with your might above those who take them captive, for those who oppress us are enemies to your holiness."
c 74:6 This Psalm also describes what the enemy of our souls has done spiritually to mar the image of God in the *inner place* of man's spirit. God will fully restore all things, including his image within us, as our hearts become his *Holy Place* on the earth.

Let's wipe out every trace of this God.
Let's burn up every sacred place
Where they worship this God."
9Now there's nothing left to show
That we are the people of God![a]
No miraculous signs anymore!
There's no longer a prophet among us
Who can tell us how long this devastation will continue!
10So God, how much longer will you let this go on
And allow these barbarians to blaspheme your name?
Will you stand back and watch them get away with this forever?
11Why don't you do something?
You have the power to break in,
So why would you hide your great power from us?
Don't hold back!
Unleash your might and give them a final blow.
12You have always been, and always will be, my King.
You are the Mighty Conqueror
Working wonders all over the world.
13It was you who split the sea in two
By your glorious strength.
You smashed the power of Tannin, the sea-god![b]
14You crushed the might of Leviathan,[c] the great dragon,
Then you took the crumbs and fed them to the sharks![d]
15With your glory you opened up springs and fountains,
Then you spoke and the ever flowing springs of Jordan
Dried up so we could cross over.
16You own the day and the night.
Sunlight and starlight call you Creator.
17The four corners of the earth were formed by your hands,
And every changing season owes its beauty to you.
18O, Jehovah, don't ever forget how these arrogant enemies,

a 74:9 Implied in the text.
b 74:13 As translated literally from the Hebrew. The Septuagint says, "You've crushed the heads of the dragons in the water [water spirits]."
c 74:14 Leviathan is mentioned six times in Job 41. Leviathan means twisted or coiled, and is considered to be a sea monster. See Genesis 1:21.
d 74:14 The Septuagint says, "You fed them to the black peoples."

Like fools, have mocked your name.
19Lord, aren't we your beloved dove that praises you?[a]
Protect us from these wild beasts who want to harm us.
Don't leave us as lambs among wolves!
You can't abandon us after all we've been through!
20Remember your promises to us,
For darkness covers the land,
Giving the violent ones a hiding place.
21Don't let these insults continue. Can't you see
That we are your downtrodden and oppressed people?
Make the poor and needy into a choir of praise to you!
22Don't ignore these ignorant words; this continual mocking.
Rise up, God; it's time to defend yourself from all of this.
23Never forget what your adversaries are saying.
For their rage and uproar rise continually against you.
It's time to stand up to them![b]

a 74:19 As translated from the Septuagint, Syriac, and one Hebrew manuscript.
b 74:23 Implied in the context.

Psalm 75

A CUP IN GOD'S HAND

To the Pure and Shining One
Asaph's poetic song to the tune "Do Not Destroy"

1God, our hearts spill over with praise to you!
We overflow with thanks, for your name is the "Near One."
All we want to talk about is your wonderful works!
And we hear your reply:
2 "When the time is ripe I will arise,
And I will judge the world with perfect righteousness!
3Though I have set the earth firmly on its pillars
I will shake it until it totters and everyone's hearts will tremble."

Pause in his presence

4God warns the proud, "Stop your arrogant boasting!"
And he warns the wicked,
"Don't think for a moment you can resist me!
5Why would you speak with such stubborn pride?
Don't you dare raise your fist against me!"
6-7This I know: the favor that brings promotion and power
Doesn't come from anywhere on earth,
For no one exalts a person but God, the true Judge of all.
He alone determines where favor rests.
He anoints one for greatness,
And brings another down to his knees.
8A foaming cup filled with judgment mixed with fury,
Is in the hands of the Lord Jehovah,
Full to the brim and ready to run over.
He filled it up for the wicked and they will drink it,
Down to the very last drop!
9But I will proclaim the victory of the God of Jacob.
My melodies of praise will make him known.[a]
10My praises will break the powers of wickedness
While the righteous will be promoted and become powerful!

a 75:9 Implied in the text.

Psalm 76

AWE-INSPIRING POWER

To the Pure and Shining One
Asaph's poetic tune, a song of smiting

1God is well-known in the land of Judah.
He is famous throughout Israel,
2Making his home in Jerusalem, living here on Mount Zion.
3That's where he smashes every weapon of war that comes against him.
That's where he uses the broken arrows
As kindling for his mighty bonfire.

Pause in his presence

4God, you are so resplendent and radiant![a]
Your majesty shines from your everlasting mountain.
Nothing could be compared to you in glory!
5Even the mightiest of men have been paralyzed by your presence.
They were so stunned and lifeless not even
The strongest one could lift a hand.
6When Jacob's God roared his rebuke, soldiers and their steeds
All fell to the ground, stunned and lying still.
7No wonder you are greatly feared! You are the awe-inspiring God!
For who could ever stand before your face
When your fierce anger burns,
And still live to tell about it.
8As the earth itself holds its breath in awe before you,
Judgment is decreed from heaven.
9You arise to punish evil and defend the gentle upon the earth.

Pause in his presence

10You have power to transform man's futile anger into praise.[b]
The fury of your enemies only causes your fame to increase.[c]

a 76:4 The Hebrew-Aramaic word used here is *anointed*.
b 76:10 Or, "the counsel of men will praise you."
c 76:10 The Septuagint reads, "survivors of your wrath keep your festivals."

11So you'd better keep every promise you've ever made
To the Awesome One, Jehovah God!
Let everyone bring their extravagant gifts to him alone.
12He is famous for breaking the spirit of the powers that be.
And the kings of the earth will know him as the Fearsome One!

Psalm 77

GOD OF COMFORT

To the Pure and Shining One
Asaph's poetic song of love's celebration

[1]I poured out my complaint to you, God.
I lifted up my voice, shouting out for your help.
[2]When I was in deep distress, in my day of trouble,
I reached out for you with hands stretched out to heaven!
Over and over I kept looking for you, God–
But your comforting grace was nowhere to be found.
[3]As I thought of you I just moaned:
"God, where are you?"[a]
I'm overwhelmed with despair
As I wait for your help to arrive.

Pause in his presence

[4]I can't get a wink of sleep until you come and comfort me.
Now I'm too burdened to even pray!
[5]My mind wanders thinking of days gone by;
The years long since passed.
[6]Then I remembered my worship songs I used to sing
In the night seasons,
And my heart began to fill again with thoughts of you.
So my spirit went out once more in search of you.
[7]Would you really walk off and leave me forever, my Lord God?
Won't you show me your kind favor; delighting in me again?
[8]Has your well of sweet mercy dried up?
Will your promises never come true?
[9]Have you somehow forgotten to show me love?
Are you so angry that you've closed
Your heart of compassion toward me?

Pause in his presence

a 77:3 Implied in the context.

10 Lord, what wounds me most is
That it's somehow my fault that
You've changed your heart toward me
And I no longer see the years of the Mighty One
and your right hand of power.[a]
11 Yet I could never forget all your miracles, my God,
As I remember all your wonders of old.
12 I ponder all you've done, Lord, musing on all your miracles.
13 It's here in your presence, in your sanctuary,
Where I learn more of your ways.[b]
For Holiness is revealed in everything you do!
Lord, you're the One and Only, the great and glorious God!
14 Your display of wonders, miracles, and power
Makes the nations acknowledge you.
15 By your glory-bursts you've rescued us over and over.
Just ask the sons of Jacob, or
The sons of Joseph and they will tell you!
And all of us, your beloved ones, know that it's true!

Pause in his presence

16 When the many waters of the Red Sea took one look at you[c]
They were afraid and ran away to hide—
Trembling to its depths!
17 Storm clouds filled with water high in the skies;
Cloudbursts and thunderclaps announced your approach.
Lightning-flashes lit up the landscape.
18 Rolling whirlwinds exploded with sonic booms of thunder,
Rumbling as the skies shouted out your story
With light and sound and wind.
Everything on earth shook and trembled as you drew near.[d]
19 Your steps formed a highway through the seas,
With footprints on a pathway no one even knew was there.[e]
20 You led your people forward by your loving hand,
Blessed by the leadership of Moses and Aaron.

a 77:10 This difficult verse has a number of alternate translations, including: "Your right hand has changed [or withered]." The implication is that God's power and protection are no longer being seen.
b 77:13 This is an alternative translation, followed by the King James Bible.
c 77:16 Although the Red Sea is not mentioned in the verse, it is implied in the context.
d 77:18 Implied in the context.
e 77:19 This could be a prophecy of Jesus one day walking on water.

Psalm 78

LESSONS FROM HISTORY

Asaph's poetic song of instruction

1Beloved ones, listen to this instruction.
Open your heart to the revelation
Of this mystery that I share with you.
2A parable and a proverb is hidden in what I say,
An intriguing riddle from the past.
3-4We've heard true stories from our fathers
About our rich heritage. We will continue
To tell our children and not hide from the rising generation
The great marvels of our God, his miracles and power
That have brought us all this far.
5The story of Israel is a lesson in God's ways.
He gave Moses his laws then commanded us to keep them,
And to make them known to all our children.
6For perpetuity God's ways will be passed down
From one generation to the next, even to those not yet born.
7In this way, every generation will have
A living faith in the laws of life
And will never forget the faithful ways of God.
8By following his ways they will break the past bondage
Of their fickle fathers who were a stubborn, rebellious generation
And whose spirits strayed from the Eternal God.
They refused to love him with all their hearts!
9Take for an example, the sons of Ephraim;
Though they were all equipped warriors, each with weapons,
When the battle began they retreated and ran away in fear.
10They didn't really believe the promises of God;
They simply refused to trust him and move forward in faith.
11They forgot his wonderful works and the miracles of the past,
12Even their exodus from Egypt, the epic miracle of his might.
They forgot the glories of his power

At the place of passing over.[a]
13God split the sea wide open, and
The waters stood at attention on either side
As the people passed on through!
14By day the moving glory-cloud led them forward.
And all through the night
The fire-cloud stood as a sentry of light.
15-16In the days of desert dryness he split open the mighty rock,
And the waters flowed like a river before their very eyes.
He gave them all they wanted to drink from his living springs.
17Yet they kept their rebellion alive against God Most High,
And their sins against God continued to be counted.
18In their hearts they tested God just to get what they wanted,
Asking for the food their hearts craved.
19-20Like spoiled children they grumbled against God himself,
Demanding he prove his love by saying,[b]
"Can't God provide for us in this barren wilderness?
Will he give us food, or will he only give us water?
Where's our meal?"
21Then God heard all their complaining and was furious!
His anger flared up against his people,
22For they turned away from faith and walked away in fear;
They failed to trust in his power to help them when he was near.
23-24Still he spoke on their behalf and the skies opened up;
The windows of heaven poured out food,
The mercy bread-manna.
The grain of grace fell from the clouds.
25Humans ate angels' food, the meal of the mighty ones.
His grace gave them more than enough!
26-27The heavenly winds of miracle power blew in their favor.
And food rained down upon them;
Succulent quail quieted their hunger
As they ate all they wanted.
28Food fell from the skies, thick as clouds;

a 78:12 Or, "the fields of Zoan." *Zoan* means crossing place or place of departure. See also verse 43.
b 78:19-20 Implied in the context.

Their provision floated down right in front of their eyes!
29He gave them all they desired, and they ate to their fill.
30-31But before they had even finished,
Even with their food still in their mouths,
God's fiery anger arose against them
Killing the finest of their mighty men.
32Yet in spite of all this, they kept right on sinning.
Even when they saw God's marvels
They refused to believe God could care for them.
33So God cut their lives short with sudden disaster,
With nothing to show for their lives but fear and failure.
34When he cared for them they ignored him,[a]
But when he began to kill them,
Ending their lives in a moment,
They came running back to God pleading for mercy.
35They remembered that God, the Mighty One,
Was their strong Protector,
The Hero-God who would come to their rescue.
36-37But their repentance lasted only
As long as they were in danger;
They lied through their teeth to the True God of Covenant.
So quickly they wandered away from his promises,
Following God with their words and not their hearts!
Their worship was only flattery.
38But amazingly, God—so full of compassion—still forgave them.
He covered over their sins with his love,
Refusing to destroy them all.
Over and over he held back his anger,
Restraining wrath to show them mercy.
39He knew that they were made from mere dust—
Frail, fragile, and short-lived,
Here today and gone tomorrow.
40How many times they rebelled in their desert days!
How they grieved him with their grumblings.
41Again and again they limited God;

a 78:34 Implied in the context.

Preventing him from blessing them.
Continually they turned back from him
And wounded the Holy One!
42They forgot his great love, how he took them by his hand
And with redemption's kiss[a]
He delivered them from their enemies.
43They disregarded all the epic signs and marvels they saw
When they escaped from Egypt's bondage.
They forgot the judgment of the plagues that set them free.
44God turned their rivers into blood, leaving the people thirsty.
45How he sent them vast swarms of
Filthy flies that sucked their blood.
He sent hordes of frogs, ruining their lives.
46And grasshoppers consumed all their crops.
47And every garden, every orchard
Was flattened with blasts of hailstones.
Their fruit trees ruined by a killing frost.
48Even their cattle fell prey, pounded by the falling hail;
Their livestock were struck with bolts of lightning.
49Finally, he unleashed upon them
The fierceness of his anger. Such fury!
He sent them sorrow and devastating trouble
By his mighty band of destroying angels;
Messengers of death were dispatched against them!
50-51He lifted his mercy and let loose his fearful anger
And did not spare their lives.
He released the judgment-plagues to rage through their land.
God struck down in death all the firstborn sons of Egypt;
The pride and joy of each family!
52Then like a Shepherd leading his sheep, God led his people
Out of tyranny, guiding them toward the Land of Promise.[b]
53Safely and carefully God led them out with nothing to fear.
But their enemies he led into the sea.
He took care of them there once and for all!
54Eventually God brought his people to the Holy Land,

a 78:42 Implied in the context.
b 78:52 Implied in the text.

To a land of hills that he prepared for them.[a]
55He drove out and scattered all the peoples occupying the land,
Staking out an inheritance,
A portion for each of Israel's tribes.
56Yet for all of this, they still rebelled
And refused to follow his ways
Provoking to anger the God Most High.
57-58Like traitors turning back they forsook him.
They were even worse than their fathers!
They became treacherous deceivers, crooked and corrupt,
And worshipped false gods in the high places,
Bringing low the name of God with every idol they erected.
No wonder he was filled with jealousy and furious with anger!
59Enraged with anger, God turned his wrath on them,
And he rejected his people with disgust!
60God walked away from them and left his dwelling place at Shiloh,
Abandoning the place where he had lived among them.
61Allowing his emblem of strength, his glory-ark to be captured,[b]
Enemies stole the very Source of Israel's power.
62God vented his rage, allowing his people to be butchered
When they went out to battle,
For his anger was intense against his very own!
63Their young men fell on the battlefield and never came back.
Their daughters never heard their wedding songs,
Since there was no one left to marry!
64Their priests were slaughtered and their widows were killed
Before they had time to weep.
65Then all at once the Almighty awakened
As though he had been asleep.
Like a mighty man he arose, roaring into action!
66He blasted into battle driving back every foe,
Defeating them in disgrace for time and eternity.
67He rejected Joseph's family, the tribe of Ephraim,[c]

a 78:54 The Aramaic reads: "He brought them to the border of his holiness, the mountain possessed by his right hand."
b 78:61 Implied in the text. Although the ark is not directly mentioned in this text, the obvious implication is that God allowed his "strength" to be stolen as a sign of his judgment.
c 78:67 The place of God's dwelling was moved from the land of Ephraim (Shiloh) to the land of Judah (Jerusalem).

68But he chose instead the tribe of Judah
And Mount Zion, which he loves.
69There he built his towering temple,
Strong and enduring as the earth itself.
70And God also chose his beloved one, David.
He promoted him from caring for sheep
And made him his prophetic servant.
71-72God prepared David and took this gentle shepherd-king
And presented him before the people
As the one who would love and care for them
With integrity, a pure heart, and the anointing
To lead Israel, his holy inheritance.

Psalm 79

PRAYER IN A TIME OF NATIONAL DISASTER

Asaph's poetic song

1God, won't you do something?
Barbarians have invaded your inheritance.
Your temple of holiness has been violated,
And Jerusalem has been left in ruins.
2The corpses of your loving people are lying in the open,
Food for the beasts and the birds.
3The shed blood of your servants has soaked the city
With no one left to bury the dead.
4Now the nearby nations heap their scorn upon us;
Scoffing, mocking us incessantly.
5How much longer, O Jehovah God, must we endure this?
Does your anger have no end?
Will your jealousy burn like a raging fire?
6If you're going to pour out your anger,
Pour it out on all these nations around us, not on us!
They're the ones that do not love you like we do!
7See how they've attacked us, consuming the land, leaving it desolate.
8Please, God, don't hold the sins of our fathers against us.
Don't make us pay for their sins.
Hurry to our side, and let your
Tenderhearted mercy meet us in our need,
For we are devastated beyond belief.
9Our Hero, come and rescue us!
O God of the Breakthrough,
For the glory of your name, come and help us!
Forgive and restore us; heal us and cover us in your love.
10Why should all the nations sneer at us saying:
"Where is this God of yours?"
Now is the time, Lord; show your people and all the world

That you will avenge this slaughter and bloodshed once and for all!
11Listen, Lord! Hear the sighing of all the prisoners of war,
All those doomed to die. Demonstrate your glory-power
And come and rescue your condemned children!
12Lord God, take what these mocking masses have done to us
And pay it all back to them seven times over.
13Then we, your lovers, will forever thank you,
Praising your name from generation to generation!

Psalm 80

RESCUE AND RESTORE

For the Pure and Shining One
Asaph's poetic song set to the tune "Your Decrees Are Like Lilies"

1God-Enthroned, be revealed in splendor, as you ride upon the cherubim!
How perfectly you lead us, a people set free.[a]
Loving Shepherd of Israel—listen to our hearts' cry!
Shine forth from your throne of dazzling light.
2Stir up your mighty power in full display before our eyes.[b]
Break through and reveal yourself by coming to our rescue,
For the sake of those who follow your glory.
3Revive us, O God! Let your beaming face shine upon us
With the sunrise rays of glory,
Then nothing will be able to stop us.
4O God, the Mighty Commander of Angel-Armies,
How much longer will you smolder in anger? How much longer
Will you be disgusted with your people even when they pray?
5You have fed us with sorrow and grief
And made us drink our tears by the bowlful.
6You've made us a thorn in the side of all the neighboring lands,
And now they just laugh at us with their mocking scorn.
7Come back, come back, O God, and restore us!
You are the Commander of Angel-Armies.
Let your beaming face shine upon us
With the sunrise rays of glory,
And then nothing will be able to stop us!
8-9Remember how you transplanted us here
Like a tender vine from Egypt.
You cleared the land for your vineyard,

a 80:1 Or, "You lead Joseph like a flock." Joseph, as a metaphor, becomes a picture of the saga of God's people once imprisoned and now set free to rule and reign.

b 80:2 The Hebrew text includes the names Ephraim ("doubly fruitful"), Benjamin ("son of my right hand"), and Manassah ("you made me forget"). These three sons of Rachel marched together behind the ark of glory (Numbers 2:17–24) and became representatives of all who follow the glory of God. They will be "doubly fruitful," "sons of his right hand," and those who have "forgotten" their lives in Adam.

Evicting the nations from your land and planting us here!
The roots of your vineyard went deep into the soil
And filled the land with fruit.
10-11Because of your favor on your vineyard, blessing extended
To every mountain of influence.
Through this flourishing vineyard mighty ones were raised up.
The nations were blessed by your fruitful vineyard of Israel,[a]
All the way from the Mediterranean to the Euphrates.
12-13So Lord, why have you broken down
Your fence of favor around us?
Trespassers can steal the fruit from off our vines,
And now every wild beast comes
Breaking through our wall to ravage us.
You've left us without protection!
14Come back, come back, O God to restore us!
You are the Commander of Angel-Armies.
Look down from heaven and see our crisis.
Come down and care for your lovely vineyard once again.
15Nurture our root and our fruit with your loving care.
Raise up the Branch-Man, the Son that you've made strong.
16Enemies chopped down our vine and set it on fire;
Now show them your anger and let them perish by your frown.
17Strengthen this Branch-Man, the Son of your love,
The Son of Man who dwells at your right hand.
18Then we will never turn back from you;
Revive us again, that we may trust in you.
19O God, the Mighty Commander of Angel-Armies,
Come back and rescue us!
Let your beaming face shine upon us with the sunrise rays of glory,
Then nothing will ever stop us again!

a 80:10-11 In this passage the translator has chosen to make explicit the symbols in the text. The vineyard is Israel; the mountains are the high places of influence in culture; the cedars are the mighty and powerful of men; and the sea speaks of the nations ("sea of humanity").

Psalm 81

FOR THE FEAST OF TABERNACLES

For the Pure and Shining One
Asaph's poetic song set to the melody "For the Feast of Harvest"

1Lord, just singing about you makes me strong!
So I'll keep shouting for joy
To Jacob's God, my Champion!
2Let the celebration begin!
I will sing with drum accompaniment,
And with the sweet sound
Of the harp and guitar strumming.
3Go ahead! Blow the jubilee trumpet to begin the feast!
Blow it before every joyous celebration and festival.[a]
4For God has given us these seasons of joy,
Days that he decreed for us to celebrate and rejoice.
5He's given these feasts
To remind us of his triumph over Egypt,
Which ended our slavery in a strange and foreign land.[b]
Then I heard the message in an unknown tongue
As he said to me:
6"I have removed your backbreaking burdens
And have freed your hands
From the hard labor and toil.[c]
7You called out to Me in your time of trouble
And I rescued you.
I came down from the realm of the secret place of thunder
Where mysteries hide.
I came down to save you.
I tested your hearts at the place

a 81:3 Or, "on the day of the new moon and the day of the full moon."
b 81:5 Implied in the text.
c 81:6 Or, "from holding the baskets," which alludes to the Hebrews carrying basket loads of burdens for their Egyptian masters.

Where there was no water to drink,
The place of your bitter argument with me."[a]

Pause in his presence

8"Listen to me, my dear people.
For I'm warning you, and you'd better listen well!
For I hold something against you.
9Don't ever be guilty of
Worshipping any other god but me.
10I am your only God, the Living God!
Wasn't I the One who broke the strongholds over you
And raised you up out of bondage?
Open your mouth with a mighty decree,
I will fulfill it now, you'll see!
The words that you speak, so shall it be!
11But my people still wouldn't listen;
My princely people would not yield to me.
12So I lifted my grace from off of their lives
And I surrendered them
To the stubbornness of their hearts,
For they were living according
To their own selfish fantasies.
13O, that my people would once and for all listen to me
And walk faithfully in my footsteps, following my ways.
14Then and only then, will I conquer your every foe
And tell everyone of them, 'You must go!'
15Those who hate my ways will cringe before me
And their punishment will be eternal.
16But I will feed you with my spiritual bread.
You will feast and be satisfied with me
Feeding on my revelation-truth like honey
Dripping from the cliffs of the high place."

a 81:7 The Hebrew includes the word *Meribah*, which means the place of strife and contention.

Psalm 82

TRUE JUSTICE

Asaph's poetic song

1All rise! For God now comes to judge
As he convenes heaven's courtroom![a]
He judges every judge and rules over every ruler! Saying,
2"How long will you judges refuse to listen
To the voice of true justice
And continue to corrupt what is right
By judging in favor of the wrong?"

Pause in his presence

3"Defend the defenseless,
The fatherless and the forgotten,
The disenfranchised and the destitute.
4Your duty is to deliver the poor and the powerless;
Liberate them from the grasp of the wicked.
5But you continue in your darkness and ignorance
While the foundations of society are shaken to the core!
6Didn't I commission you as judges, saying,
'You are all like gods, since you judge on my behalf.
You are all like sons of the Most High, my representatives.'
7Nevertheless, in death you are nothing but mere men!
You will be laid in the ground like any prince and you will die."
8All rise! For God now takes his place as Judge of all the earth!
Don't you know that everything and everyone belongs to him?
The nations will be sifted in his hands!

a 82:1 The Aramaic says, "God now stands in the assembly of the angels, and he will judge in their midst."

Psalm 83

GOD, DON'T BE SILENT [a]

Asaph's poetic song

1God, you have to do something![b]
Don't be silent and just sit idly by.
2–3Can't you see what they're doing?
All your enemies are stirred up in an uproar!
They despise you, Lord!
In their defiant arrogance they rise up
To host their secret council against your people.
They conspire together to come and harm
Your cherished ones—your hidden ones.
4Our enemies keep saying,
"Now is the time to wipe Israel off the map.
We'll destroy even the memory of her existence!"
5They've made their pact;
Consulting and conspiring,
Aligning together in their covenant against God!
6-8All the sons of Ishmael, the desert sheiks and
The nomadic tribes, Amalekites, Canaanites, Moabites,
And all the nations that surround us,
Philistines, Phoenicians, Gadarenes,[c] and Samaritans;
Allied together they're ready to attack!

Pause in his presence

9Do to them all what you did
To the Midianites who were defeated by Gideon.
Or what you did to Sisera and Jabin
When Deborah and Barak defeated them by the Kishon River.
10Do to your enemies what you did at Endor,
Whose rotting corpses fertilized the land.

a The historical background to this Psalm may be found in 2 Chronicles 20:14–36.
b 83:1 Both the Aramaic and the Septuagint add a line in verse 1: "God, who is like you?"
c 83:6–8 As translated from the Aramaic.

11-12Repeat history, God! Make all their "noble ones"
Die like Oreb, Zebah, and Zalmunna, who said in their pride,
"We will seize God's people along with all their pleasant lands!"
13Just blow them away, God, like straw in the wind,
Like a tumbleweed in the wilderness!
14Burn them up like a raging fire
Roaring down the mountainside;
Consume them all until only charred sticks remain!
15Chase them away like before a
Mighty storm and terrifying tempest!
16O Lord, disgrace them until their faces fill with shame,
And make them acknowledge the glory of your name!
17Make them utter failures in everything they do
Until they perish in total disgrace and humiliation.
18So that they will know that you, and you alone
Are Yahweh, the only Most High God
Exalted over all the earth!

Psalm 84

LONGING FOR GOD

For the Pure and Shining One

A prophetic song written by the sons of Korah
Set to the melody "For the Feast of Harvest"[a]

1God of Heaven's Armies,
You find so much beauty in your people!
They're like lovely sanctuaries of your presence.[b]
2So deep within me are these lovesick longings,
Desires and daydreams of living in union with you.
When I'm near you my heart and my soul
Will sing and worship with my joyful songs of you,
My true Source and Spring of life!
3O Lord of Heaven's Armies, my King and my God,
Even the sparrows and swallows are welcome to build a nest
Among your altars for the birds to raise their young.
4What pleasure fills those who live every day in your temple,
Enjoying you as they worship in your presence!

Pause in his presence

5How enriched are they who find their strength in the Lord;[c]
Within their hearts are the highways of holiness!
6Even when their path winds through the dark valley of tears,
They dig deep to find a pleasant pool
Where others find only pain.[d]
He gives to them a brook of blessing
Filled from the rain of an outpouring.
7They grow stronger and stronger
With every step forward,

a The Septuagint says, "For the wine vats."
b 84:1 The Hebrew word for lovely used here can also mean beloved. The translator has chosen to use both these concepts in this verse.
c 84:5 The Aramaic says, "How blessed is the Son of Man with you as his helper."
d 84:6 Implied in the context.

Until they find all their strength in you,[a]
And the God of all gods will appear before them in Zion.
8Hear my cry, O God of Heaven's Armies!
God of Jacob, listen to my loving prayer.

Pause in his presence

9God, your wrap-around presence is our defense.
In your kindness look upon
The faces of your anointed ones.[b]
10For just one day of intimacy with you[c] is like
A thousand days of joy rolled into one!
I'd rather stand at the threshold
In front of the Gate Beautiful,
Ready to go in and worship my God,
Than to live my life without you
In the most beautiful palace of the wicked.
11For the Lord God is brighter
Than the brilliance of a sunrise!
Wrapping himself around me like a shield,
He is so generous with his gifts of grace and glory.
12Those who walk along his paths with integrity
Will never lack one thing they need,
For he provides it all!
O Lord of Heaven's Armies,
What euphoria fills those
Who forever trust in you!

a 84:7 Implied in the context.
b 84:9 Or, "the face of your Anointed [Christ]."
c 84:10 Or, "in your [temple] courts."

Psalm 85

MERCY AND TRUTH

For the Pure and Shining One
A prophetic song composed by the sons of Korah

1Lord, your love has poured out
So many amazing blessings on our land!
You've restored Israel's destiny from captivity.
2You've forgiven our many sins and covered
Every one of them in your love.

Pause in his presence

3So now it's obvious that your blazing anger has ended,
And the furious fire of wrath has been extinguished by your mercy.[a]
4So bring us back to loving you, God our Savior.
Restore our hearts so that we'll never again
Feel your anger rise against us.
5Will you forever hold a grudge?
Will your anger endure for all time?
6Revive us again, O God! I know you will! Give us a fresh start!
Then all your people will taste your joy and gladness.
7Pour out even more of your love on us!
Reveal more of your kindness and restore us back to you!
8Now I'll listen carefully for your voice
And wait to hear whatever you say.
Let me hear your promise of peace,
The message every one of your godly lovers longs to hear.
Just don't let us in our ignorance turn back from following you.
9For I know your power and presence shines on all your lovers.
Your glory always hovers over all who bow low before you.
10Your mercy and your truth have married each other.
Your righteousness and peace have kissed.

a 85:3 Implied in the text.

11 Flowers of your faithfulness are blooming on the earth.
Righteousness shines down from the sky.
12 Yes, the Lord keeps raining down blessing after blessing,
And prosperity will drench the land with a bountiful harvest.
13 For deliverance and peace are his forerunners
Preparing a path for his steps.

Psalm 86

A PRAYER OF FAITH

King David's prayer

1Lord, bend down to listen to my prayer.
For I'm in deep trouble. I'm so broken and humbled,
And I desperately need your help.
2Guard my life, for I'm your faithful friend,
Your loyal servant for life.
I turn to you in faith, my God,
My Hero, come and rescue me!
3Lord God, hear my constant cry for help,
Show me your favor and bring me to your fountain of grace!
4Restore joy to your loving servant once again,
For all I am is yours, O God.
5Lord, you are so good to me, so kind in every way[a]
And ready to forgive,
for your grace-fountain keeps overflowing,
Drenching all your lovers who pray to you.
6God, won't you pay attention to this urgent cry?
Lord, bend down to listen to my prayer.
7Whenever trouble strikes I will keep crying out to you,
For I know your help is on the way.
8God, there's just no one like you—
There's no other god as famous as you.
You outshine all others,
And your miracles make it easy to know you.
9Lord Almighty, you are the One who created all the nations;
Look at them—they're all on their way!
Yes, the day will come when they all will worship you,
And put your glory on display.
10You are the one and only God!

a 86:5 The Septuagint says, "You're my Provider."

What miracles! What wonders!
What greatness belongs to you!
11Teach me more about you;
How you work and how you move,
So that I can walk onward in your truth,
Until everything within me brings honor to your name.
12With all my heart and passion I will thank you, my God!
I will give glory to your name, always and forever!
13You love me so much,
And you placed your greatness upon me.[a]
You rescued me from the deepest place of darkness,
And you have delivered me from a certain death.
14God, look at how these arrogant ones have defied me.
Like a vicious band of violent men they have tried to kill me.
They wouldn't worry for moment
That they were sinning against you!
15But Lord, your nurturing love is tender and gentle.
You are slow to get angry, yet so swift to show your faithful love,
You are full of abounding grace and truth.[b]
16Bring me to your grace-fountain
So that your strength becomes mine.
Be my Hero and come rescue your servant once again!
17Send me a miraculous sign to show me
How much you love me,
So that those who hate me will see it and be ashamed.
Don't they know that you, Lord, are my Comforter,
The One who comes to help me!

a 86:13 As translated from the Aramaic.
b 86:15 As translated from the Aramaic and the Septuagint.

Psalm 87

FOUNTAINS OF JOY

A prophetic song, composed by the sons of Korah

1High upon his hills of holiness stands God's city![a]
2How God loves Zion, his favorite place on earth.[b]
3So many glorious things have been proclaimed
Over Zion, God's holy city!

Pause in his presence

4For the Lord says, "Here are the nations
Who will acknowledge me as God:[c]
Egypt,[d] Iraq,[e] Palestine,[f] and the Mediterranean people,[g]
Even distant Ethiopia! They will all boast,
'I was born in Zion!'"
5But over Zion it will be said:
The Mighty Man was born there and he will establish it![h]
For the God Most High will truly bless Jerusalem.
6And when he counts her citizens, recording them in his registry,
He will write by their name: "This one was born again here!"

Pause in his presence

7And the princes of God's feasts will sing and dance,[i]
Singing, "Every fountain of delight springs up
From your life within me!"

a 87:1 The Aramaic reads, "His foundations are in his holy mountains."
b 87:2 Or, "The Lord loves Zion's gates more than all the dwelling places of Jacob."
c 87:4 This is in anticipation of the nations of the earth coming to know Christ as the eternal King. See also Psalm 86:9.
d 87:4 Or, "The proud one," which is a title given to Egypt. See Isaiah 30:7.
e 87:4 Or, "Babyon," which means gate of god.
f 87:4 Or, "Philistia," which means land of sojourners.
g 87:4 Or, "Tyre," which means a rock.
h 87:5 As translated from the Aramaic. The Hebrew reads, "Each one is born in Zion and the Most High makes her secure."
i 87:7 As translated from the Armaic.

Psalm 88

SAVE ME FROM THIS SORROW[a]

To the Pure and Shining One
A prophetic song for the sons of Korah
To the tune "Pierced" for instruction by Heman the Ezrahite

1Yahweh is the God who continually saves me.
I weep before you night and day.
2Please bend down and listen to my sobbing,
For my life is riddled with troubles
And death is just around the corner!
3Everyone sees my life ebbing out.
They just consider me a hopeless case,
And see me as a dead man.
4They've all left me here to die,
Helpless, like one who is doomed for death.
5They're convinced you've forsaken me,
Certain that you've forgotten me completely—
Abandoned, pierced, with nothing
To look forward to but death.
6They[b] have discarded me,
And thrown me down into the deepest darkness,
As into a bottomless pit.
7I feel your wrath and it's a heavy weight upon me,
Drowning me beneath a sea of sorrow.

Pause in his presence

8Why did you turn all my friends against me?
You've made me like a cursed man in their eyes.
No one wants to be with me now.
You've caught me in a trap with no way out.
9Every day I beg for your help.

a This psalm has traditionally been used by Christians for reading on Good Friday. Many insights can be found here of the crucifixion of Jesus Christ.
b 88:6 As translated from the Septuagint. The Hebrew reads, "You have discarded me."

Can't you see my tears?
My eyes are swollen with weeping.
My arms are wide, longing for mercy,[a]
But you're nowhere to be found.
Soon it will be too late![b]
10How can those who are cut off from your care
Even know that you are there?
How can I rise up to praise you if I'm dead and gone?

Pause in his presence

11Who can give thanks for your love in the graveyard?
Who preaches your faithfulness in the place of destruction?
12Does death's darkness declare your miracles?
How can anyone who's in the grave, where all is forgotten,
Remember how you keep your promises?
13Lord, you know my prayer before I even whisper it.[c]
At each and every sunrise you will
Continue to hear my cry until you answer.
14God, why are you treating me like this?[d]
Why have you thrown my life away?
Will you keep turning the other way
Every time I call out to you?
15I've had to live in poverty and trouble all my life.[e]
Now I'm humiliated, broken, and helpless before your terrors;
And I can't take it anymore.
16I'm so overwhelmed by your burning anger.
I've taken the worst you could give me
And I'm speechless before you.
17I'm drowning beneath the waves of this sorrow,
Cut off with no one to help.
18All my loved ones and friends keep far away from me,
Leaving me all alone with only darkness as my friend!

a 88:9 As translated from the Septuagint. The Greek reads, "My hands are stretched out to you."
b 88:9 Implied in the context.
c 89:13 As translated from the Septuagint.
d 88:14 Implied in the context.
e 89:15 As translated from the Septuagint. The Greek reads, "close to death all my life."

Psalm 89

WILL YOU REJECT US FOREVER?

Poems by Ethan the Ezrahite for instruction[a]

First poem—God's Promises to David

1This forever-song I sing
Of the gentle love of God overwhelming me!
Young and old alike will hear about
Your faithful, steadfast love, never failing!
2Here's my chorus: "Your mercy grows through the ages.[b]
Your faithfulness is firm, rising up to the skies."
3I heard the Lord say, "My covenant has been made,
And I'm committed forever to my chosen one, David.
4I have made my oath that there will be sons of David forever,
Sons that are kings through every generation."

Pause in his presence

5-6Can you hear it? Heaven is filled with your praises, O Lord!
All the holy ones are praising you for your miracles!
The sons of God are all praising you for your mighty wonders.
We could search the skies forever and never find one like you.
All the mighty angels could not be compared to you.
7You are a God who is greatly to be feared
As you preside over the council of holy ones.
You are surrounded by trembling ones
Who are overwhelmed with fear and dread,
Stunned as they stand in awe of you!
8So awesome are you, O Yahweh, Lord God of Angel-Armies!
Where could we find anyone as glorious as you?
Your faithfulness shines all around you!
9You rule over oceans and the swelling seas.

a Many scholars believe Psalm 89 contains four poems or stanzas. The translator has chosen to signify each poem with an inscription.
b 89:2 As translated from the Septuagint.

When their stormy waves rise, you speak, and they lie still.[a]
10You crushed the strongholds of Egypt,
And all your enemies were scattered
At the mighty display of your glory-power.
11All the heavens and everything on earth belong to you
For you are the Creator of all that is seen and unseen.
12The four corners of the earth were put in place by you.
You made the majestic mountains
That are still shouting their praises to your name.
13Breathtaking and awesome is your power! So astounding and
Unbelievable is your might and strength when it goes on display!
14Your glorious throne rests on a foundation
Of righteousness and just verdicts.
Grace and truth are the attendants who go before you.
15The happiest people on earth
Are those who worship you with songs.
They firmly march along shouting with joy and
Shining in the radiance streaming from your face.
16We can do nothing but leap for joy all day long;
For we know who you are and what you do,
And you've exalted us on high.
17The glory of your splendor is our strength,
And your marvelous favor makes us even stronger,
Lifting us even higher!
18You are our King, the Holiest One of all;
Your wrap-around presence is our protection!

Second poem—God Keeps His Promises

19-20You spoke to your prophets in visions, saying—
"I have found a mighty hero for my people.
I have chosen David as my loving servant and exalted him.
I have anointed him as king with the oil of my holiness.
21I will be strength to him and I will give him
My grace to sustain him no matter what comes.
22"None of his enemies will get the best of him,

a 89:9 This could be a prophecy of Jesus who would one day calm the stormy seas.

Nor will the wicked one overpower him.
23For I will crush his every adversary
And do away with all who hate him!
24Because I love him and treasure him,
My faithfulness will always protect him.
I will place my great favor upon him,
And I will cause his power and fame to increase.
25David's kingdom shall reach from
The Mediterranean to the Euphrates River.
26And he will come before me, saying—
'You truly are my Father, my only God, and my strong Savior!'
27I am setting him apart, favoring him as my firstborn son.
I will make him like unto me, the most high king in all the earth!
28I will love him forever and always show him kindness.
My covenant with him will never be broken.
29For I have decreed that he will always have an heir;
A dynasty that will release the days of heaven on earth.
30-32But if his children turn from me and forsake my words, refusing
To walk in my truth, renouncing and violating my laws, then I will surely
Punish them for their sins with my stern discipline until they regret it!
33But I will never, no never, lift my faithful love from off their lives.
My kindness will prevail and I will never disown them.
34-35How could I revoke my covenant of love that I promised David?
For I have given him my word, My holy irrevocable word!
How could I lie to my loving servant David?
36-37Sons of David will continue to reign on his throne,
And their kingdom will endure as long as the sun is in the sky.
This covenant will be an unbreakable promise that
I have established for all time!"

Pause in his presence

Third poem—Why Has Our King Been Defeated

38Why have you rejected me, the one you anointed?
Why would you cast me away?
Why would you lose your temper with me?
39You have torn up the contract you made with me, your servant.

You have stripped away my crown and thrown it to the ground.[a]
40You have torn down all my walls of defense
And have made my every hiding place into ruins.
41All the passersby attack and rob me while my neighbors mock!
42Instead of fighting for me, you took the side of my enemies,
Even giving them strength to subdue me,
And then watched them celebrate their victory!
43You are no longer helping me in battle. You've forsaken me
To the swords of those who would strike me down.
44You've made my regal splendor to decrease
And allowed my rule to be overthrown.
45Because of you, I've become old before my time and
I'm publicly disgraced!

Pause in his presence

Fourth poem—"Save Me, God"

46How long will you hide your love from me?
Have you left me for good?
How long will your anger continue to burn against me?
47Remember, Lord, I am nothing but dust,
Here today and so soon blown away.
Is this all you've created us for? For nothing but this?
48Which one of us will live forever?
We are all mortal, terminal, for we will all one day die.
Which one of us would ever escape our appointment with death
And dodge our own funeral?

Pause in his presence

49So God, where is all this love and kindness you promised us?
What happened to your covenant with David?
50Have you forgotten how your own servants are being slandered?
Lord God, it seems like I'm carrying in my heart
All the pain and abuse of your forgotten ones.
51They have relentlessly insulted and persecuted us,
Your anointed ones.
52Nevertheless, blessed be our God forever and ever.
Amen; faithful is our King!

a 89:39 In place of the word *crown*, some translations render it "my dignity."

BOOK IV

The "Numbers" Psalms

PSALMS OF OUR PILGRIMAGE ON EARTH

Psalm 90

GOD, THE ETERNAL

A prayer of Moses, God's prophet

1Lord, come be our eternal Home,
Our hiding place from generation to generation.
2Long before you gave birth to the earth,
And before the mountains were born,
You have been from everlasting to everlasting,[a]
The One and Only true God.
3When you speak the words:
"Life, return to me!"
Man turns back to dust.
4 One thousand years pass before your eyes,
Like yesterday that quickly faded away,
Like a night's sleep so soon forgotten.[b]
5-6 One day we will each be swept away
Into the sleep of death!
We glide along through the tides of time—
So quickly gone, like a dream that fades at dawn.[c]
Like glistening grass that springs up one day
And is dry and withered the next, ready to be cut down!
7Terrified by your anger,
Confined beneath the curse,
We live our lives knowing your wrath.[d]
8For all of our faults and flaws are in full view to you![e]
Everything we want to hide, you search out
And expose by the radiance of your face.
9We are banished to live in the shadow of your anger.
Our days soon become years,

a 90:2 The Hebrew word for *eternity* is actually *horizon*—from one horizon to the other!
b 90:4 Or, "like divisions [watches] of the night."
c 90:5–6 A poetic description of what is implied in the context.
d 90:7 Or, "worn out by your rage." Jesus has come and broken the curse and lifted the unbearable burden of our sins.
e 90:8 The Septuagint reads, "The laws we have broken all stand before you."

Until our lifetime comes to an end,
Finished with nothing but a sigh.[a]
10You've limited our life span to a mere seventy years,
Yet some you give grace to live still longer.[b]
But even the best of years are marred by
Tears and toils, and in the end with nothing more
Than a gravestone in a graveyard![c]
We're gone so quickly, so swiftly,
We pass away and simply disappear.
11Lord, who fully knows the power of your passion
And the intensity of your emotions?[d]
12Help us to remember that our days are numbered;
And help us to interpret our lives correctly.
Set your wisdom deeply in our hearts
So that we may accept your correction.[e]
13Return to us again, O God! How much longer will it take,
Until you show us your abundant compassion?
14Let the sunrise of your love end our dark night.
Break through our clouded dawn again!
Only you can satisfy our hearts, filling us with songs of joy
To the end of our days.
15We've been overwhelmed with grief;
Come now and overwhelm us with gladness!
Replace our years of trouble with decades of delight!
16Let us see your miracles again, and let the rising generation
See the glorious wonders you're famous for.
17O Lord our God, let your sweet beauty rest upon us, and give us favor.
Come work with us, and then our works will endure,
And give us success in all we do!

a 90:9 The Septuagint reads, "All our days have been filled with failures."
b 90:10 Or, "if in strength eighty years."
c 90:10 A poetic description of what is implied in the context. The Septuagint has the phrase, "until we mellow and accept your correction."
d 90:11 As translated from the Aramaic. The Hebrew can be translated, "Who could experience the strength of your anger? Who could endure the fear your fury can bring, and who truly comprehends the fear of God?"
e 90:12 As translated from the Septuagint.

Psalm 91

SAFE AND SECURE

1When you sit enthroned[a] under the shadow of Shaddai,[b]
You are hidden[c] in the strength of God Most High.
2Here's how I describe him:
He's the hope that holds me, and the Stronghold to shelter me,
The only God for me, and my great Confidence.
3And he will rescue you from every hidden trap of the enemy,[d]
And he will protect you from false accusation
And any deadly curse.[e]
4His massive arms[f] are wrapped around you, protecting you.
You can run under his covering of majesty and hide.
His arms of faithfulness are a shield keeping you from harm.
5You will never worry about an attack of demonic forces at night,
Nor have to fear a spirit of darkness coming against you.
6Don't fear a thing! Whether by night or by day,
Demonic danger will not trouble you,[g]
Nor the powers of evil launched against you.
For God will keep you safe and secure; they won't lay a hand on you![h]
7Even in a time of disaster with thousands and thousands being killed,
You will remain unscathed and unharmed!
8You will be a spectator as the wicked perish in judgment,
For they will be paid back for what they have done!

a 91:1 Or, "O, you who sits enthroned." The Hebrew word *yoseb* is often associated with one seated as royalty. It is translated in Ezekiel 27:8 as leaders or rulers.

b 91:1 *Shaddai* (*šadday*) is taken from a Hebrew root word with many expressive meanings. It can mean, "God of the Mountain, God the Destroyer of Enemies, God the Self-Sufficient One, God the Nurturer of Babies, God the Almighty."

c 91:1 Or, "I endure through the night." See Job 39:28 where the same Hebrew word is used for an eagle passing the night on the high cliffs.

d 91:3 Or, "hunter."

e 91:3 As translated from the most ancient Hebrew manuscripts and the Septuagint. The Hebrew word can mean poisoned arrows.

f 91:4 Or, "wings." Also found in the next sentence, "under his wings," which speaks not of God having wings, but his wings of the cherubim resting on the mercy seat. The implication is that you can always come to the mercy seat and rest without fear.

g 91:6 Verses 5–6 are seen by many Jewish scholars as a reference not merely to pestilence and natural dangers, but to the realm of spiritual darkness that would come against God's servants. These spirits are equated to"arrows that fly in daytime" or a "pestilence that walks" in the darkness. God's sheltered ones are kept from the harm that could come from natural sources or supernatural sources. What a wonderful place to hide and be secure!

h 91:6 Implied in the context.

9-10 When we live our lives within the shadow
Of the God Most High, our secret Hiding Place,
We will always be shielded from harm!
How then could evil prevail against us, or disease infect us?
11God sends angels with special orders
To protect you wherever you go,
Defending you from all harm.
12If you walk into a trap they'll be there for you
And keep you from stumbling!
13You'll even walk unharmed
Among the fiercest powers of darkness,[a]
Trampling every one of them beneath your feet!
14For here is what the Lord has spoken to me:
"Because you have delighted in me as my great lover,
I will greatly protect you.
I will set you in a high place,
Safe and secure before my face.
15I will answer your cry for help every time you pray,
And you will find and feel my presence
Even in your time of pressure and trouble.
I will be your glorious Hero and give you a feast!
16You will be satisfied with a full life
And with all that I do for you.
For you will enjoy
The fullness of my salvation!"

a 91:13 The Hebrew includes the words for *lions, snakes*, and *dragon* as the three great symbols of satanic power.

Psalm 92

A SUNDAY MORNING SONG OF PRAISE

A poetic praise song for the day of worship[a]

[1]It's so enjoyable to come before you,
With uncontainable praises spilling from our hearts!
How we love to sing our praises over and over to you,
To the matchless God, high and exalted over all!
[2]At each and every sunrise we will be thanking you
For your kindness and your love.
As the sun sets and all through the night
We will keep proclaiming, "You are so faithful!"
[3]Melodies of praise will fill the air
As every musical instrument,[b] joined with every heart,
Overflows with worship.
[4]No wonder I'm so glad, I can't keep it in!
Lord, I'm shouting with glee over all you've done,
For all you've done for me!
[5]What mighty miracles and your power at work,
Just to name a few!
Depths of purpose and layers of meaning
Saturate everything you do.
[6]Such amazing mysteries found within every miracle,
That nearly everyone seems to miss.
Those with no discernment can never really discover
The deep and glorious secrets hidden in your ways!
[7]It's true the wicked flourish, but only for a moment,
Foolishly forgetting their destiny with death,
That they will all one day be destroyed forevermore.
[8]But you, O Lord, are exalted forever

a Ancient Jewish tradition holds that Adam composed this Psalm on the first Sabbath of creation, and it was to be sung by the Levites on the Sabbath in the temple.
b 92:3 Or, "a ten-stringed harp and lyre."

In the highest place of endless glory,
9While all your opponents, the workers of wickedness,
They will all perish, forever separated from you!
10Your anointing has made me strong and mighty.
You've empowered my life for triumph[a]
By pouring fresh oil over me!
11You've said that those lying in wait to pounce on me
Would be defeated, and now
It's happened right in front of my eyes
And I've heard their cries of surrender!
12Yes! Look how you've made all your lovers
To flourish like palm trees,
Each one growing in victory, standing with strength![b]
13You've transplanted them into your heavenly courtyard
Where they are thriving before you.
14For in your presence they will still overflow and be anointed.
Even in their old age they will stay fresh,
Bearing luscious fruit and abiding faithful.
15Listen to them! With pleasure they still proclaim:
"You're so good! You're my beautiful Strength!
You've never made a mistake with me!"

a 92:10 Implied in the text. The Septuagint reads, "I will raise my horn high like a rhinoceros [Hebrew translated to *wild ox*], and in my old age I will still have plenty of oil [anointing]."
b 92:12 Or, "growing high like a cedar in Lebanon." God makes us immortal and immovable.

Psalm 93

THE MAJESTY OF GOD

A Friday song,
composed by King David after being resettled in the land [a]

1Look! Yahweh now reigns as King!
He has covered himself with majesty and strength,
Wearing them as his splendor-garments!
Regal power surrounds him
As he sits securely on his throne.
He's in charge of it all, the entire world,
And he knows what he's doing!
2Lord, you have reigned as King
From the very beginning of time.
Eternity is your home.
3-4Chaos once challenged you.
The raging waves lifted themselves over and over,
High above the ocean's depths, letting out their mighty roar!
Yet at the sound of your voice
They were all stilled by your might.
What a majestic King, filled with power!
5Nothing could ever change your royal decrees;
They will last forever!
Holiness is the beauty that fills your house;
You are the One who abides forevermore!

a This inscription is found in the Septuagint. Jews called this Psalm "The Friday Psalm." The Talmud indicates that this Psalm was sung every Friday in the temple by the Levites.

Psalm 94

GOD OF VENGEANCE

A Wednesday song composed by King David [a]

1Lord God Almighty, you are the God
Who takes vengeance on your enemies!
It's time for you to punish evil!
Let your rays of revelation-light shine from your people and
Pierce the conscience of the wicked and punish them!
2It's time to arise as Judge of all the earth;
Arise to punish the proud with the penalty they deserve!
3How much longer will you sit back and watch the wicked
Triumph in their evil, boasting in all that is wrong?
4–5Listen to them bragging among themselves,
Big in their own eyes, all because of the crimes
They've committed against your people!
See how they're crushing those who love you, God,
Cruelly oppressing those who belong to you.[b]
6Heartlessly they murder the widows, the foreigners,
And even the orphaned children.
7They say to themselves,
"The Lord God doesn't see this.
Their God, the God of Jacob, he doesn't even care!"
8But you'd better watch out, you stupid fools!
You'd better wise up! Why would you act like God doesn't exist?
Do you really think that God can't hear their cries?
9God isn't hard of hearing; he'll hear all their cries!
God isn't blind! He who made the eye has superb vision,
And he's watching all you do.
10Won't the God who knows all things know what you've done?
The God who punishes nations will surely punish you!

a This inscription is taken from the Septuagint. The Mishnah states that this Psalm was sung by the Levites on the fourth day of the week, each Wednesday, in the temple.
b 94:4–5 Or, "[the people of] his inheritance." See also verse 14.

11The Lord has fully examined every thought of man
And found them all to be empty and futile.
12Lord Yah, there's such a blessing that comes
When you teach us your Word and your ways.[a]
Even the sting of your correction can be sweet.
13It rescues us from our days of trouble
Until you are ready to punish the wicked.[b]
14For the Lord will never walk away from his cherished ones,
Nor would he forsake his chosen ones who belong to him.[c]
15Whenever you pronounce judgments they reveal righteousness.[d]
All your lovers will be pleased, because the future belongs to them.[e]
16Lord, who will protect me from these wicked ones?
If you don't stand to defend me, who will? I have no one but you!
17I would have been killed so many times
If you had not been there for me.
18When I screamed out, "Lord, I'm doomed!"
Your fiery love was stirred and you raced to my rescue.
19Whenever my doubts and fears were out of control,
The soothing comfort of your presence
Calmed me down and overwhelmed me with delight.
20It's obvious to all; you will have nothing to do
With corrupt rulers who pass laws that empower evil
And defeat what is right.
21For they gang up against the lovers of righteousness
And condemn the innocent to death.
22-23But I know that all their evil plans will
Boomerang back onto them!
Every plot they hatch will simply seal their own doom!
For you, my God, you will destroy them,
Giving them what they deserve.
For you are my true Tower of Strength,
My Safe Place, my Hideout, and my true Shelter.

a 94:12 Or, "from your Torah."
b 94:13 Or, "until a pit is dug for the wicked."
c 94:14 Or, "[the people of] his inheritance."
d 94:15 Or, "justice will prevail."
e 94:15 Implied in the text. The Hebrew reads, "and after it [judgment] are the pure in heart."

Psalm 95

IT'S TIME TO SING

[1]Come on, everyone! Let's sing for joy to the Lord!
Let's shout our loudest praises to our God, who saved us!
[2]Everyone come meet his face with a thankful heart!
Don't hold back your praises,
Make him great by your shouts of joy!
[3]For the Lord is the greatest of all!
King-God over all other gods!
[4]In one hand he holds the mysteries of the earth
And in the other he holds the highest mountain peaks!
[5]He's the owner of every ocean,
The Engineer and Sculptor of earth itself!
[6]Come and kneel before this Creator-God;
Come and bow before the mighty God, our majestic Maker!
[7-9]For we are the lovers he cares for, and he is the God we worship!
So drop everything else and listen to His voice!
For this is what he's saying:
"Today, when I speak, don't even think about turning a deaf ear to me,
Like they did when they tested me at Meribah and Massah,[a]
The place where they argued with me, their Creator.
Your ancestors challenged me
Over and over with their complaining,
Even though I had convinced them of my power and love,
Yet they still doubted my care for them.
[10]So for forty long years I was grieved and disgusted by them.
I described them as wicked wanderers,
Whose hearts would not follow my ways or keep my Words!
[11]So I made a vow in my anger and declared:
'They will never enter the resting place I've planned for them!'
So don't you ever be hard-hearted
Or stubborn like they were!"[b]

a 95:7–9 *Meribah* means strife, argument. *Massah* means testing.
b 95:11 Implied in the context and made explicit for the sake of English narrative.

Psalm 96

KING OF THE WORLD

1Go ahead—sing your new song to the Lord!
Let everyone in every language sing him a new song.[a]
2–3Don't stop! Keep on singing! Make his name famous!
Tell everyone every day how wonderful he is!
Give them the good news of our great Savior.
Take the message of his glory and miracles to every nation.
Tell them about all the amazing things he has done.
4For the Lord's greatness is beyond description,
And he deserves all the praise that comes to him.
He is our King-God, and it's right to be in holy awe of him.
5Other gods are absolutely worthless.[b]
For the Lord God is Creator God, who spread the splendor of the skies!
6Breathtaking brilliance and awe-inspiring majesty
Radiate from his shining presence.
His stunning beauty overwhelms all who come before him![c]
7Surrender to the Lord Yahweh all you nations and peoples.
Surrender to him all your pride and strength.
8Confess that Jehovah alone deserves all the glory and honor!
Bring an offering and come celebrate in his courts.
9Come worship the Lord God wearing the splendor of holiness.
Let everyone wait in wonder as they tremble in awe before him.
10Tell the nations plainly that Yahweh rules over all!
He is doing a great job, and nothing will disrupt him,
For he treats everyone fair and square.
11–12Let the skies sing for joy! Let the earth join in the chorus.
Let oceans thunder and fields echo this ecstatic praise,
Until every swaying tree of every forest joins in,
Lifting up their songs of joyous praise to him!
13For here he comes, the Lord God, and he's ready to judge the world.
He will do what's right and can be trusted to always do what's fair!

a 96:1 Every new thing God does requires a new song to make it known.
b 96:5 The Septuagint reads "demons."
c 96:6 Or, "strength and beauty are in his sanctuary."

Psalm 97

GOD RULES OVER ALL

A psalm of David when his kingdom was established[a]

1Yahweh now reigns as King! Let everyone rejoice!
His rule extends everywhere, even to distant lands,
And the islands of the sea, let them all be glad!
2Clouds both dark and mysterious now surround him.[b]
His throne of glory rests upon
A foundation of righteousness and justice.
3All around him burns a blazing glory-fire
Consuming all his foes.
4When his lightning strikes, flashing in the skies,
People are wide-eyed, as they tremble and shake.
5Mountains melt away like wax in a fire
When the Lord of all the earth draws near!
6Heaven's messengers preach righteousness and
People everywhere see his glory in the sky!
7Shame covers all who boast in other gods,
For they worship idols.
For all the supernatural powers
Once worshipped the true and Living God!
8But God's Zion-people are content,
For they know and hear the truth.
The people of praise rejoice
Over all your judgments, O Lord!
9For you are King-God,
The Most High God over all the earth.
You are exalted above every supernatural power!
10Listen, you lovers of God, hate evil;
For God can keep you from wrong
And protect you from the power of wickedness.

a This inscription is from the Septuagint.
b 97:2 See also Deuteronomy 4:11 and 5:22.

11 For he sows seeds of light within his lovers,
Releasing a harvest in the souls of the righteous.
Seeds of joy burst forth for the lovers of God!
12 So be glad, and continue to give him thanks,
For God's holiness is seen in everything he does.

Psalm 98

SING A NEW SONG

David's poetic praise [a]

1Go ahead—sing your brand-new song to the Lord!
He is famous for his miracles and marvels.
For he is victorious through his mighty power and holy strength.
2Everyone knows how God has saved us,
For he has displayed his justice throughout history.
3He never forgets to show us his love and faithfulness.
How kind he has been to Israel!
All the nations know how he stands behind his people
And how he saves his own.
4So go ahead everyone and shout out your praises with joy!
Break out of the box and let loose
With the most joyous sound of praise!
5Sing your melody of praise to the Lord,
And make music like never before![b]
6Blow those trumpets and shofars!
Shout with joyous triumph before King Yahweh!
7Let the ocean's waves join in the chorus
With their roaring praise,
Until everyone everywhere shouts out in unison:
"Glory to the Lord!"
8Let the rivers and streams clap with applause
As the mountains rise in a standing ovation
To join the mighty choir of exaltation!
9Look! Here he comes! The Lord and Judge of all the earth!
He's coming to make things right and to do it fair and square.
And everyone will see that he does all things well!

a The Septuagint has David as the author. The Hebrew says simply "A Psalm."
b 98:5 Or, "accompanied by a harp and the sound of music."

Psalm 99

GOD OF HOLINESS

1 Yahweh is King over all!
Everyone trembles in awe before him!
He rules enthroned between the wings of the cherubim.
So let the earth shake and quake in wonder before him!
2 For Yahweh is great and glorious in the midst of his Zion-people.
He is exalted above all!
3 Let everyone praise this breathtaking God, for he is holy!
4 A lover of justice is our mighty King;
He is right in all his ways.
He insists on being fair to all,
Promoting true justice and equity throughout Israel.
5 So everyone, exalt the Lord our God,
Facedown before his glory-throne,
For he is great and holy!
6 In times of crisis God has his praying priests,[a]
Like Moses, Aaron, and Samuel, who all interceded
Asking God for help.
God heard their cries and came to their rescue.
7 He spoke to them from the pillar of clouds
And they followed his instructions,
Doing everything he told them.
8 God, the great Forgiver,
Answered their prayers.
Yet he would punish them when they went astray.
9 Keep exalting the Lord our God,
Facedown before his glory-throne,
For he is great and holy!

a 99:6 Implied in the text.

Psalm 100

PRAISE GOD

A poetic song for thanksgiving

1Lift up a great shout of joy to the Lord!
Go ahead and do it—
Everyone, everywhere!
2As you serve him bring your gift of laughter[a]
And be glad as you worship him.
Sing your way into his presence with joy!
3And realize what this really means—
We have the privilege of worshipping the Lord, our God.
For he is our Creator,
And now we belong to him!
We are the people of his pleasure.[b]
4You can pass through his open gates
With the password of praise.
Come right into his presence with thanksgiving.
Come bring your thank-offering to him
And affectionately bless his beautiful name!
5For the Lord is always good
And ready to receive you.
He's so loving that it will amaze you;
So kind that it will astound you!
And he is famous for his faithfulness toward all.
Everyone knows our God can be trusted,
For he keeps his promises to every generation!

a 100:2 Implied in the context.
b 100:3 Or "the sheep of his pasture."

Psalm 101

INTEGRITY

David's poetic praise

1Lord, I will sing about your faithful love for me!
My song of praise will have your justice as its theme.
2I'm trying my best to walk in the way of integrity,
Especially in my own home.
But now I need your help!
I'm wondering, Lord, when will you appear?
3I refuse to gaze on that which is vulgar.
I despise what is evil,
And anything that moves my heart away from you.
I will not let evil hold me in its grip.
4Every perverse and crooked way,
I have put away from my heart;
For I will have nothing to do with the deeds of darkness.[a]
5I will silence those who secretly want to slander my friends,
And I will not tolerate the proud and arrogant.
6My innermost circle will only be those
That I know are pure and godly.
They will be the only ones I allow to minister to me.
7There's no room in my home for hypocrites,
For I can't stand chronic liars who flatter and deceive.
8At each and every sunrise I will awake to do what's right,
And put to silence those who love wickedness,
Freeing God's people[b] from their evil grip.
I will do all of this because of my great love for you![c]

a 101:4 Or, "evil people."
b 101:8 Or, "the city of Yahweh."
c 101:8 This phrase, though not found in the Hebrew text, brings conclusion to the Psalm and is implied in the context.

Psalm 102

FROM TEARS TO PRAISE

A prayer for those who are overwhelmed and for all the discouraged who come to pour out their hearts before the Lord[a]

1Lord, listen to my prayer! Listen to my cry for help!
2You can't hide your face from me in the day of my distress.
Stoop down to hear my prayer and answer me quickly, Lord!
3-4For my days of happiness have gone up in smoke.
My body is raging with fever, my heart is sick, and I'm consumed
By this illness—withered like a dead leaf and I can't even eat.
5I'm nothing but skin and bones.
Nothing's left of me but whispered groans.
6I'm depressed, lonely, forgotten, and abandoned.[b]
7I'm sleepless, shivering in the cold, forlorn and friendless
Like a lonely bird on the rooftop.
8My every enemy mocks and insults me incessantly.
They even use my name as a curse to speak over others!
9-10Because of your great and furious anger against me
All I do is suffer with sorrow, with nothing to eat
But a meal of mourning.[c] My crying fills my cup with salty tears!
In your wrath you have rejected me,
Sweeping me away like dirt on the floor.
11My days are marked by the lengthening shadows of death.
I'm withering away and there's nothing left of me.
12But then I remember that you, O Lord,
Still sit enthroned as King over all!
The fame of your name will be revealed to every generation!
13I know you are about to arise and show your tender love to Zion.
Now is the time Lord, for your compassion and mercy

a As translated from the Septuagint.

b 102:6 The Hebrew makes reference to a "pelican" or "vulture" in the wilderness, and "an owl in desolate ruins." The translator has chosen to use the obvious meanings of the metaphors.

c 102:9–10 Or, "I eat ashes as if they were bread." Ashes speak of mourning, for mourners would often throw dust and ashes over their heads.

To be poured out—the appointed time has come
For your prophetic promises to be fulfilled![a]
14For your servants weep in sympathy over Zion's ruins
And feel love for her every stone.
15When you arise to intervene, all the nations and kings will be stunned
And will fear your awesome name, trembling before your glory!
16Yes, you will reveal yourself to Zion
And appear in the brightness of your glory,
To restore her and give her children.
17He responds to the prayer of the poor and broken
And will not despise the cry of the homeless.
18Write all this down for the coming generation,
So the born-again people[b] will read it and praise the Lord!
19Tell them how Yah[c] looked down from his high and holy place,
Gazing from his glory to survey the earth.
20He listened to all the groaning of his people longing to be free,
And set loose the sons of death to experience life.
21Multitudes will stream to Jerusalem to
Praise the Lord and declare his name in Zion!
22Peoples from every land, their kings and kingdoms,
Will gather together to worship the Lord!
23But God has brought me to my knees, shortening my life.
24So I cry out to you, my God, the Father of eternity,
Please don't let me die! I know my life is not yet finished!
25With your hands you once formed the foundations of the earth
And handcrafted the heavens above.
26-27They will all fade away one day like worn-out clothing
Ready to be discarded, but you'll still be here.
You will replace it all!
Your first creation will be changed, but you alone
Will endure, the God of all eternity!
28Generation after generation our descendants will live securely,
For you are the One protecting us, keeping us for yourself.

a 102:13 Implied in the context.
b 102:18 Or, "those born anew [re-created]."
c 102:19 Taken from *Yahweh*. Yah is often used as the name of the God of Power.

Psalm 103

OUR FATHER'S LOVE

King David's song of praise

1With my whole heart, with my whole life,
And with my innermost being,
I bow in wonder and love before you, the Holy God!
2Yahweh, you are my soul's celebration;
How could I ever forget the miracles of kindness you've done for me?
3You kissed my heart with forgiveness, in spite of all I've done.[a]
You've healed me inside and out from every disease.
4You've rescued me from hell[b] and saved my life.
You've crowned me with love and mercy and made me a king.[c]
5You satisfy my every desire with good things.[d]
You've supercharged my life so that I soar again,[e]
Like a flying eagle in the sky!
6You're a God who makes things right,
Giving justice to the defenseless.
7You unveiled to Moses your plans
And showed Israel's sons what you could do.
8You're so kind and tenderhearted to those who don't deserve it,
And so very patient with people who fail you!
Your love is like a flooding river overflowing its banks with kindness.
9You don't look at us only to find our faults,
Just so that you can hold a grudge against us.
10You may discipline us for our many sins,
But never as much as we really deserve.
Nor do you get even with us for what we've done.
11Higher than the highest heavens—

a 103:3 Starting from this verse and through the rest of the Psalm, the writer shifts to the second person (you). The translator has chosen to leave the Psalm in the first person to enhance the poetic nuance for the English reader.
b 103:4 Or "redeemed me from the pit," a term often used for Sheol or hell.
c 103:4 Implied in the context of King David's poetic song of placing crowns on our heads.
d 103:5 The Hebrew text is somewhat difficult to understand. It is literally "who satisfies with good ornaments."
e 103:5 Or "your youth [implying both strength and beauty] he restores."

That's how high your tender mercy extends!
Greater than the grandeur of heaven above
Is the greatness of your loyal love,
Towering over all who fear you and bow down before you!
12Farther than from a sunrise to a sunset;
That's how far you've removed our guilt from us!
13The same way a loving father feels toward his children;
That's but a sample of your tender feelings toward us,
Your beloved children, who live in awe of you!
14You know all about us inside and out.
You are mindful that we're made from clay.
15Our days are so few, and
Our momentary beauty[a] so swiftly fades away!
16Then all of a sudden we're gone, like grass clippings
Blown away in a gust of wind,
Taken away to our appointment with death,
Leaving nothing to show that we were here.
17But Lord, your endless love stretches from one eternity to the other,
Unbroken and unrelenting toward those who fear you
And those who bow facedown in awe before you!
Your faithfulness to keep every gracious promise you've made
Passes from parents, to children, to grandchildren, and beyond.
18You are faithful to all those who follow your ways and keep your Word.
19God's heavenly throne is eternal, secure, and strong,
And his kingdom rules the entire universe!
20So bless the Lord, all his messengers of power,
For you are his mighty heroes
Who listen to the voice of his Word to do it!
21Bless and praise the Lord, you mighty warriors,
Ministers who serve him well and fulfill his desires!
22I will bless and praise the Lord with my whole heart!
Let all his works throughout the earth,
Wherever his dominion stretches,
Let everything bless the Lord!

a 103:15 The Hebrew word translated *beauty* actually means "shining."

Psalm 104

OUR CREATOR'S COMPASSION[a]

1Everything I am will praise and bless the Lord!
O Lord, my God, your greatness takes my breath away,
Overwhelming me by your majesty, beauty, and splendor![b]
2You wrap yourself with a shimmering, glistening light.
You wear sunshine like a garment of glory.
You stretch out the starry skies like a tapestry.
3You build your balconies with light beams
And ride as King in a chariot you made from clouds.
You fly upon the wings of the wind.
4You make your messengers into winds of the Spirit,
And all your ministers become flames of fire.
5You, our Creator, formed the earth; and
You hold it all together so it will never fall apart.
6You poured the ocean depths over the planet,
Submerging mountains beneath.
7Yet at the sound of your thunder-shout
The waters all fled away, filling the deep with seas!
8The mountains rose and valleys sank
To the levels you decreed for them.
9Then you set a boundary line for the seas,
And commanded them not to trespass.
10You sent springs cascading through the valleys,
Flowing freely between the mountains and hills.
11You provide drink for every living thing;
Men and beasts[c] have their thirst quenched because of you.

a This Psalm, attributed to David in the Septuagint, can be seen as an exposition of the days of creation:
1st Day: verses 1–2
2nd Day: verses 3–4
3rd Day: verses 5–17
4th Day: verses 18–23
5th Day: verses 24–26
6th Day: verses 21–30

b 104:1 See Job 40:10.

c 104:11 Or, "wild donkeys."

12The birds build nests near the tranquil streams,
Chirping their joyous songs from the branches above.
13From your kindness you send the rain to water the mountains
From the upper rooms of your palace.
Your goodness[a] bring forth fruit for all to enjoy.
14Your compassion brings the earth's harvest, feeding the hungry.
You cause the grass to grow for livestock, along with the
Fruit, grains, and vegetables to feed mankind.
15You provide sweet wine to gladden hearts.
You give us daily bread to sustain life,
Giving us glowing health for our bodies.[b]
16The trees of the Lord drink until they're satisfied.
Lebanon's lofty trees stand tall right where you planted them.
17Within their branches you provide for birds
A place to build their nests;
Even herons find a home in the cypress trees.
18You make the high mountains a home for wild goats,
And the rocky crag where the rock badgers burrow.
19You made the moon to mark the months
And the sun to measure the days.
20You turn off the light and it becomes night,
And all the beasts of the forest come out to prowl.
21The mighty lions roar for their dinner,
But it's you, God, who feeds them all!
22At sunrise they slink back to their dens
To crouch down in the shadows.
23Then man goes out to his labor and toil,
Working from dawn to dusk.
24O Lord, what an amazing variety of all you have created!
Wild and wonderful is this world you have made,
While Wisdom was there at your side!
This world is full of so many creatures, yet each belongs to you!
25And then there is the sea! So vast! So wide and deep!
Swarming with countless forms of sea life, both small and great!
26Trading ships glide through the high seas,

a 104:13 Or, "your works."
b 104:15 Or, "oil for our faces to shine."

And look! There are the massive whales bounding upon the waves.
27All the creatures wait expectantly for you
To give them their food as you determine.
28You come near and they all gather around,
Feasting from your open hands,
And each is satisfied from your abundant supply.
29But if you were to withhold from them and turned away,
Then they all would panic.
And when you choose to take away their breath,
Each one dies and returns to the dust.
30When you release your Spirit-Wind, life is created,
Ready to replenish life upon the earth.
31May God's glorious splendor endure forever!
May the Lord take joy and pleasure in all that he has made!
32For the earth's Overseer has the power to make it tremble;
Just a touch of his finger and volcanos erupt
As the earth shakes and melts.
33I will sing my song to the Lord as long as I live!
Every day I will sing my praises to God.
34May you be pleased with every sweet thought I have about you,
For you are the source of my joy and gladness!
35Now, let all the sinners be swept from the earth.
But I will keep on praising you, my Lord,
With all that is within me;
My joyous, blissful shouts of "Hallelujah"
Are all because of you!

Psalm 105

GOD'S WONDERFUL WORKS[a]

1Go ahead—and give God thanks
For all the glorious things he has done!
Go ahead and worship him!
Tell everyone about his wonders!
2Let's sing his praises! Sing, and put all of his miracles to music!
3Shine and make your joyful boast in him, you lovers of God.
Let's be happy and keep rejoicing no matter what.
4Seek more of his strength! Seek more of him!
Let's always be seeking the light of his face!
5Don't you ever forget his miracles and marvels.
Hold to your heart every judgment he has decreed.
6For you are his servants, the true seed of Abraham, and
You are the chosen ones, Jacob's sons.
7For he is the Lord our God, and
His wise authority[b] can be seen in all he does.
8-9For though a thousand generations may pass away,
He is still true to his word.
He has kept every promise[c] he made to Abraham and to Isaac.
10His promises have become an everlasting covenant to Jacob,
Confirmed to Israel's tribes.
11He said to them, "I will give you all the land of Canaan
As your inheritance."
12They were only so very few in number
When God gave them that promise,
And they were all foreigners to that land.
13They were wandering from one land to another
With no permanent home.[d]

a The first fifteen verses of this Psalm were sung as the ark of glory was brought up to Jerusalem. See 2 Samuel 6 and 1 Chronicles 13–16.
b 105:7 Or, "judgments."
c 105:8–9 Or, "promise of the covenant [pact]."
d 105:13 Implied in the context. Or, "from a kingdom to another nation."

14Yet God would not permit anyone to touch them,
Punishing even kings who came against them.
15He said to them, "Don't you dare lay a hand on my anointed ones,
And don't do a thing to hurt my prophets!"
16So God decreed a famine upon Canaan land,
Cutting off their food supply.
17But he had already sent a man ahead of his people to Egypt;
It was Joseph, who was sold as a slave.
18His feet were bruised by strong shackles,
And his soul was held by iron.
19God's promise to Joseph purged his character
Until it was time for his dreams to come true.
20Eventually, the king of Egypt sent for him,
Setting him free at last.
21Then Joseph was put in charge of everything under the king;
He became the master of the palace over all of the royal possessions.
22Pharoah gave him authority over all the princes of the land,
And Joseph became the teacher of wisdom to the king's advisors.
23Then Jacob, with all of Joseph's family,
Came from Canaan to Egypt, and settled in Goshen.[a]
24God made them very fruitful, and they multiplied incredibly,
Until they were greater in number than those who ruled them.
25God turned their hearts to hate his people,
And to deal treacherously with his servants.
26But he sent them his faithful servant, Moses, the deliverer,
And chose Aaron to accompany him.
27Their command brought down signs and wonders,
Working miracles in Egypt.
28By God's direction, they spoke and released a plague
Of thick darkness over the land.
29God turned their rivers to blood, causing every fish to die.
30And the judgment-plague of frogs came in enormous numbers,
Swarming everywhere, even into Pharaoh's bedroom!
31God spoke and another plague was released—
Massive swarms of flies, vast clouds of insects, covered the land.

a 105:23 Or, "lived as a foreigner in the land of Ham [Egypt]." Ham was a son of Noah.

32God rained down hail and flaming fire upon Egypt.
33Their gardens and vines were all destroyed,
Shattering trees into splinters throughout the territory.
34God spoke, and devouring hordes of locusts swept over the land,
35Picking the ground clean of vegetation and crops.
36Then God struck down their firstborn sons,
The pride and joy[a] of every Egyptian family.
37At last, God freed all the Hebrews from their slavery,
And sent them away laden with the silver and gold of Egypt.
And not even one was feeble[b] on their way out!
38Egypt was relieved at their exodus, ready to see them go,
For the terror of the Lord of the Hebrews had fallen upon them!
39God spread out a cloud as shade as they moved ahead,
And a cloud of fire to light up their night.
40Moses prayed and God brought them quail to eat.
He satisfied them with heaven's bread falling from the sky.
41He broke open the boulder and the waters
Poured out like a river in the desert.
42For God could never forget
His holy promise to his servant, Abraham.
43So God brought out his chosen ones with singing;
For with a joyful shout they were set free!
44He gave them lands and nations, just like he promised.
Fruitful lands of crops they had never planted were now theirs!
45All this was done for them so that they would be faithful
To keep the ways of God, obeying his laws
And following his truths. Hallelujah! Praise the Lord!

a 105:36 Or, "the beginning of all their strength."
b 105:37 Or, "not one of his tribes was a pauper." Or, "not one stumbled."

Psalm 106

GOD IS GOOD

1Hallelujah! Praise the Lord!
Everyone, thank God, for he is good and easy to please!
Your tender love for us, Lord, continues on forever.
2Who could ever fully describe your glorious miracles?
Yahweh, who could ever praise you enough?
3The happiest one on earth is the one who keeps your Word,
And clings to righteousness every moment.
4So remember me, Lord, as you take joy in your people.
And when you come to bring the blessings of salvation,
Don't forget me!
5Let me share in the wealth and beauty of all your lovers,
And rejoice with your nation in all their joys
And let me share in the glory you give to your chosen ones.
6We have all sinned so much, just like our fathers.
"Guilty" is written over our lives.
7Our fathers who were delivered from Egypt didn't fully
Understand your wonders, and they took you for granted.
Over and over you showed them such tender love and mercy!
Yet they were barely beyond the Red Sea
When they rebelled against you.
8Nonetheless, you saved them more than once,
So they would know how powerful you are,
Showing them the honor of your name.
9You roared over the waters of the Red Sea,
Making a dry path for your people to cross through.
10You freed them from the strong power of those that oppressed them,
And rescued them from bondage.
11Then the waters rushed over their enemies and drowned them all—
Not one survived.
12Seeing this, the people believed your words, and
They all broke out with songs of praise!

13Yet how quickly they forgot your miracles of power.
They wouldn't wait for you to act when they were hungry,
14But demanded you satisfy their cravings and give them food!
They tested you to the breaking point.
15So you gave them what they wanted to eat,
But their souls starved away to nothing!
16They became envious of Moses and Aaron, your holy ones.
17You split open the earth and it swallowed up
Dathan and Abiram along with their followers.
18Fire fell from heaven and burnt up all the band of rebels,
Turning them to ashes.
19They made an idol of a calf at Sinai,
And bowed to worship their man-made statue.
20They preferred the image of a grass-eating ox
To the presence of the glory-filled God.
21-22They totally forgot it was you that saved them
By the wonders and awesome miracles you worked in Egypt.
23So you were fed up and decided to destroy them,
But Moses, your chosen leader,
Stood in the gap between you and the people
And made intercession on their behalf,
To turn away your wrath from killing them all.
24Yet they still didn't believe your words
And they despised the land of delight you gave to them.
25They grumbled and found fault with everything
And closed their hearts to your voice.
26So you gave up and swore to them
That they would all die in the desert,
27And you scattered their children
To distant lands to die as exiles.
28Then our fathers joined the worshippers of the false god named
"Lord of the Pit." They even ate the sacrifices offered to the dead!
29All they did made you burn with anger.
It made you so angry that a plague broke out among them!
30It continued until Phineas intervened and executed
The guilty for causing judgment to fall upon them.[a]

a 106:30 This is implicit information found in the story of Phineas (Numbers 25:8–9).

31Because of this deed of righteousness,
Phineas will be remembered forever.
32Your people also provoked you to wrath
At the stream called Strife.[a]
This is where Moses got into serious trouble!
33Because the people were rebellious against you,
Moses exploded in anger
And spoke to them out of his bitterness.
34Neither did our fathers destroy the enemies in the land
As you had commanded them.
35But they mingled themselves with their enemies
And learned to copy their works of darkness.
36They began to serve their gods and bow before their idols;
All of this led them away from you
And brought about their downfall.
37They even sacrificed their little children to the demon spirits,
38-39Shedding the innocent blood of their sons and daughters.
These dark practices greatly defiled
The land and their own souls,
Through the murder and bloodshed of their own babies!
Their sins made them spiritual adulterers before you.
40This is why you were furious—
As your anger burned hot against them,
You couldn't even stand to look
At your very own people any longer!
41So you turned them over to the crushing hands of other nations,
And those who hated them became tyrants over them.
42Oppressive enemies subdued them,
Ruling over them with their tyranny.
43Many times you would have come to rescue them
But they continued in their rebellious ways,
Choosing to ignore your warnings.
Then they sank lower and lower, destroyed by their depravity.
44-45Yet even so, you waited and waited, watching to see
If they would turn and cry out to you for a Father's help.[b]

a 106:32 The word used here is *Meribah*, the Hebrew word for strife (Numbers 20:1–13).
b 106:44–45 Implied in the text.

And then, when you heard their cry you relented,
And you remembered your covenant
And you turned your heart toward them again,
According to your abundant, overflowing, and limitless love.
46Then you caused even their oppressors
To pity them and show them compassion!
47Do it again, Lord! Save us, O Lord, our God!
Gather us from our exile and unite us together
So that we will our give great and joyous thanks to you again,
And bring you glory by our praises!
48Blessed be our Lord God forever and ever.
And let everyone everywhere say, "Hallelujah!"
Amen! Faithful is our King!

Book V

The "Deuteronomy" Psalms

PSALMS OF PRAISE AND THE WORD

Psalm 107

GOD'S CONSTANT LOVE

1Let everyone give all their praise and thanks to the Lord!
For here's why—he's better than anyone could ever imagine.
Yes, he's always so loving and kind, and it never ends.
2–3So, go ahead—let everyone know it!
Tell the world how he broke through
And delivered you from the power of darkness and
Has gathered us together from all over the world.
He has set us free to be his very own!
4Some of us once wandered in the wilderness like desert nomads
With no true direction or dwelling place—
5Starving, thirsting, staggering;
We became desperate and filled with despair.
6Then we cried out, "Lord, help us! Rescue us!"
And he did!
7He led us right into a place of safety and abundance,
A suitable city to dwell in.
8So lift your hands and thank God for his marvelous kindness
And for all his miracles of mercy for those he loves.
9How he satisfies the souls of thirsty ones,
And fills the hungry with all that is good!
10Some of us once sat in darkness,
Living in the dark shadows of death.
We were prisoners to our pain, chained to our regrets.
11For we rebelled against God's Word and rejected
The wise counsel of God Most High.
12So he humbled us through our circumstances,
Watching us as we stumbled,
With no one there to pick us back up.
Our own pain became our punishment.
13 Then we cried out, "Lord, help us! Rescue us!"
And he did!

14His light broke through the darkness and
He led us out in freedom from death's dark shadow,
And snapped every one of our chains.
15So lift your hands and give thanks to God for his marvelous kindness
And for his miracles of mercy for those he loves!
16For he smashed through heavy prison doors and
Shattered the steel bars that held us back, just to set us free!
17Some of us were such fools, bringing on ourselves
Sorrow and suffering all because of our sins.
18Sick and feeble, unable to stand the sight of food,
We drew near to the gates of death.
19 Then we cried out, "Lord, help us! Rescue us!"
And he did!
20God spoke the words, "Be healed,"
And we were healed,
Delivered from death's door!
21So lift your hands and give thanks to God
For his marvelous kindness
And for his miracles of mercy for those he loves!
22Bring your praise as an offering and
Your thanks as a sacrifice,
As you sing your story of miracles with a joyful song!
23Some of us set sail upon the sea to faraway ports,
Transporting our goods from ship to shore.
24We were witnesses of God's power out in the ocean deep;
We saw breathtaking wonders upon the high seas.
25For when God spoke he stirred up a storm,
Lifting high the waves with hurricane winds.
26-27Ships were tossed by swelling sea, rising to the sky,
Then dropping down to the depths,
Reeling like drunkards, spinning like tops,
Everyone at their wits' end,
Until even sailors despaired of life, cringing in terror.
28 Then we cried out, "Lord, help us! Rescue us!" And he did!
29God stilled the storm, calmed the waves,
And he hushed the hurricane winds to only a whisper.
30We were so relieved, so glad as he guided us

Safely to harbor in a quiet haven.
31So lift your hands and give thanks to God for his marvelous kindness
And for his miracles of mercy for those he loves!
32Let's exalt him on high and lift up our praises in public;
Let all the people, and the leaders of the nation know
How great and wonderful is Yahweh, our God!
33Whenever he chooses he can dry up a river [a]
And turn the land into a desert,
34Or he can take a fruitful land and make it into a saltwater swamp,
All because of the wickedness of those who dwell there.
35But he also can turn a barren wilderness into an oasis with water!
He can make springs flow into desert lands,
36And turn them into fertile valleys so that cities spring up
And He gives it all to those who are hungry.
37They can plant their fields and vineyards there,
And reap a bumper crop and gather a fruitful harvest.
38God will bless them and cause them to multiply and prosper.
39But others will become poor, humbled
Because of their oppression, tyranny, and sorrows.
40For God pours contempt upon
Their arrogant abuse of power;
Heaping scorn upon their princes and
Makes them wander among ruins.
41But He raises up the poor and lowly with His favor
Giving them a safe place to live where no one can touch them!
God will grant them a large family and bless them!
42The lovers of God will rejoice when they see this.
Good men are glad when the evil ones are silenced.
43If you are truly wise, you'll learn from what I've told you!
It's time for you to consider these profound lessons
Of God's great love and mercy!

a 107:33 Implied in the context.

Psalm 108

A PRAYER FOR GOD'S HELP

A poetic psalm by King David

1 My heart, O God, is quiet and confident all because of you.
Now I can sing my song with passionate praises!
2 Awake, O my soul, with the music of his splendor.
Arise my soul and sing his praises!
I will awaken the dawn with my worship,
Greeting the daybreak with my songs of light![a]
3 Wherever I go I will thank you.
All the nations they will hear
My praise songs to you.
4 Your love is so extravagant,
It reaches higher than the heavens!
Your faithfulness is so astonishing,
It stretches to the skies!
5 Lord God, be exalted as you soar throughout the heavens.
May your shining glory be seen high above all the earth!
6 Come to your beloved ones and gently draw us out!
Answer our prayer for your saving help.
Come with your might and strength, for we need you Lord![b]
7-8 Then I heard the Lord speak in His holy splendor,
And from His sanctuary I heard the Lord promise:
"In My triumph I will be the One
To measure out the portion of My inheritance to My people,
And I will secure the land as I promised you."[c]
9 "Shechem, Succoth, Gilead, Manasseh;
They are all still Mine!" He says.
"Judah will continue to produce kings and lawgivers;

a 108:2 Implied in the text.
b 108:6 Implied in the text.
c 108:7-8 The Hebrew includes two geographical places in the text: Shechem and Succoth. Shechem is where Jacob (Israel) first bought title to the land, paying one hundred pieces of silver for the place where he camped. Succoth is another place where Jacob temporarily camped in the Land of Promise. These two places speak of God being the One who brought them in and portioned out the land for his people.

And Ephraim will produce great warriors.
Moab will become my lowly servant!
Edom will likewise serve my purposes!
I will lift up a shout of victory over the land of Philistia!
10"But who will bring my triumph into Edom's fortresses?"[a]
11Lord, have you really rejected us,
Refusing to fight our battles?
12Give us a Father's help when we face our enemies.
For to trust in any man is an empty hope.
13With God's help we will prevail with might and power.
And with God's help we'll trample down our every foe!

a 108:10 *Edom* is a variant form of the word *Adam*.

Psalm 109

GOD, IT'S TIME FOR VENGEANCE

To the Pure and Shining One
A poetic song by King David

1God of all my praise, don't stand silently by, aloof to my pain,
2While the wicked slander me with their lies.
Even right in front of my face they lie through their teeth.
3I've done nothing to him, but he still surrounds me
With his venomous words of hatred and vitriol.
4Though I love him, he stands accusing me like satan
For what I've never done.
I will pray until I become prayer itself.[a]
5He continually repays me with evil when I show him good!
He gives me hatred when I give him love!
6-7Show him how it feels! Let accusing liars be raised up against him,
Like satan himself standing right next to him.
And let him be declared "Guilty" by a wicked judge!
May even his prayers be seen as sinful!
8Shorten his life, and let another replace him!
9Make his wife a widow and his children orphans!
10Let them wander as beggars in the street,
Like homeless vagabonds, evicted from their ruins!
11Let the creditors seize his entire estate,
And strangers, like vultures, take all that's left!
12Let no one be kind to him by showing pity to his fatherless children!
13May all his posterity die with him! Cut down his family tree!
14-15And may all the sins of his ancestors be recorded,
Remembered before you, forever!
Cut off even the memory of his family from the face of the earth,
16Because he never once showed love or kindness to others,
But persecuted the poor, the brokenhearted, and afflicted ones,

a 109:4 In the face of accusation and slander, David says literally in Hebrew, "I am prayer!"

Even putting them to death!
17Since he enjoyed cursing them,
May all his curses now come raining back on him,
Until it all overwhelms him with misfortune!
Since he refused to bless others,
God, withhold every single blessing from him!
18Bitterness, such vile vindictiveness, was upon everything he did.
Cursing was his lifestyle.
19-20So smother him now with his own curses as his just reward.
This will be the Lord's punishment upon him and
All my lying accusers who speak evil against me.
21But now, O Yahweh-God, make yourself real to me
Like you promised me you would![a]
Because of your constant love and your
Heart melting kindness, come be my Hero and deliver me!
22I'm so broken, needy and hurting.
My heart is pierced through and I'm so wounded.
23I'm slipping down a dark slope,
Shaken to the core, and helpless!
24All my fasting has left me so weak I can hardly stand.
Now I'm shriveled up; nothing but skin and bones.
25I'm the example of failure and shame to all who see me.
They just walk by me shaking their heads!
26You have to help me, O Lord God!
My true Hero, come to my rescue and save me,
For you are so loving and kind!
27Then everyone will know that you have won my victory,
And they will all say, "It is finished!"
28So let them curse me if they want,
But I know you will bless me!
All their efforts to destroy me will fail,
But I will succeed and be glad!
29So let my satan-like accusers fail!
Make them look ridiculous
If they try to come against me!

a 109:21 The Hebrew text states, "for your name's sake."

Clothe them with a robe of guilty shame from this day on!
30But I will give my thanks to you over and over,
And everyone will hear my lavish praises.
31For you stand right next to the broken one
As their saving Hero to rescue them from all their accusers!

Psalm 110

MESSIAH, KING, AND PRIEST [a]

King David's psalm

1Jehovah-God said to my Lord, the Messiah:
"Sit with me as Enthroned Ruler while I subdue your every enemy.
They will bow low before you
As I make them a footstool for your feet!"[b]
2Messiah, I know God himself will establish your kingdom,
As you reign in Zion-glory.
For he says to you: "Rule in the midst of your enemies!"
3Your people will be your love offerings
Like living sacrifices spilled out before you!
In the day of your mighty power you will be exalted,
And in the brightness of your holy ones you will shine,
As an army arising from the dawning rays of a new day,
Anointed with the dew of your youth!
4Jehovah-God has taken a solemn oath,
And will never back away from it, saying:
"You are a priest for eternity, my King of righteousness!"[c]
5The Lord stands in full authority,[d]
To shatter to pieces the kings who stand against you
On the day He displays his terrible wrath.
6He will judge every rebellious nation,
Filling their battlefield with corpses,
And will shatter the strongholds of ruling powers.
7Yet he himself will drink from his inheritance
As from a flowing brook;
Refreshed by love he will stand victorious!

a This Psalm is applied to Christ in the New Testament where it is quoted more often than any other Old Testament passage.
b 110:1 A footstool symbolizes what is subdued. It is taken from the root word "to subdue."
c 110:4 The Hebrew text includes the word *Melchizedek*, the name of a Canaanite king and priest over the Jebusite kingdom that later became Jerusalem. The name *Melchizedek* means, "my king of righteousness."
d 110:5 The Hebrew word used here for *Lord* is *Adonai*, or *Adonay*. It is the plural form of *Adhon*. Jesus is called Lord of lords, and we are the lords that he is Lord over. We are seated at his right hand (Benjamin) to rule with him.

Psalm 111

CELEBRATE GOD'S GREATNESS

1Shout Hallelujah to Yahweh!
May every one of his lovers hear
My passionate praise to him;
Even among the council of the holy ones!
2For God's mighty miracles astound me!
His wonders are so delightfully mysterious,
That they leave all who seek them astonished.
3Everything he does is full of splendor and beauty!
Each miracle demonstrates his eternal perfection.
4His unforgettable works of surpassing wonder
Reveal his grace and tender mercy.
5He satisfies all who love and trust him,
And he keeps every promise he makes.
6He reveals mighty power and marvels to his people
By handing them nations as a gift!
7All God accomplishes is flawless, faithful, and fair;
And his every word proves trustworthy and true.
8They are steadfast forever and ever,
Formed from truth and righteousness.
9His forever-love paid a full ransom for his people,
So that now we're free to come before Jehovah
To worship his holy and awesome name!
10Where can wisdom be found?
It is born in the fear of God.
Everyone who follows his ways
Will never lack his living-understanding.
And the adoration of God
Will abide throughout eternity!

Psalm 112

THE TRIUMPH OF FAITH

[1]Shout in celebration of praise to the Lord!
Everyone who loves the Lord and delights in him
Will cherish his words and be blessed beyond expectation!
[2]Their descendants will be prosperous and influential.
Every generation of his godly lovers will experience his favor!
[3]Great blessing and wealth fills the house of the wise,[a]
For they will walk in the way of the righteous.
[4]Even if darkness overtakes them, sunrise-brilliance
Will come bursting through,
Because they are gracious to others, so tender and true.
[5]Life is good for the one who is generous and charitable,
Conducting affairs with honesty and truth.
[6]Their circumstances will never shake them,
And others will never forget their example.
[7]They will not live in fear or dread of what may come,
For their hearts are firm, ever secure in their faith.
[8]Steady and strong they will not be afraid,
But will calmly face their every foe,
Until they all go down in defeat.
[9]Never stingy and always generous to those in need,
Their lives of influence and honor will never be forgotten
For they were full of good deeds!
[10]But the wicked take one look at a life lived like this
And they grit their teeth in anger,
Not understanding their bliss.
The wicked slink away speechless in the darkness that falls,
Where hopes dies, and all their dreams
Fade away to nothing,
To nothing at all!

a 112:3 Implied in the context.

Psalm 113

GOD IS KIND

1Hallelujah! Praise the Lord![a]
Go ahead—praise the Lord
All you loving servants of God!
Keep it up! Praise him some more!
2For the glorious name of the Lord is
Blessed forever and ever.
3From sunrise brilliance to sunset beauty,
Lift up his praise from dawn to dusk!
4For he rules on high over the nations,
With a glory that outshines even the heavens.
5No one can be compared to God, enthroned on high!
He stoops down to look upon the earth and the skies.
6He promotes the poor, picking them up from the dirt,
7And rescues the wretched ones
From utter degradation and despair,
Restoring to them their destiny.[b]
8He turns paupers into princes and seats them
On their royal thrones of honor.
9God's grace provides for the barren ones
A joyful home with children,
So that even childless couples find a family.
He makes them happy parents
Surrounded by their pride and joy.
That's the God we praise,
So give it all to him!

a 113:1 Psalms 113–114 were sung before the meal, during the Jewish family's celebration of Passover, while Psalms 115–118 were sung after the meal (see Mark 14:26).
b 113:7 Implied in the context.

Psalm 114

A SONG FOR PASSOVER

1Many years ago the Jewish people escaped Egypt's tyranny,
2So that Israel, God's people of praise,[a]
Would become his holy sanctuary,
His kingdom on the earth.
3The Red Sea waters saw them coming
And ran the other way!
Then later, the Jordan River too,
Moved aside so that they could all pass through.
4The land shuddered with fear as they moved ahead.
Mountains and hills shook with dread,
As the people of God stepped forward![b]
5O Sea, what happened to you, to make you flee?
O Jordan, what was it that made you turn and run?
6O mountains, what frightened you so?
And you Hills, what made you shiver?
7Tremble, O Earth, for you are in
The presence of the Lord!
God now appears with his people.[c]
8He splits open boulders
And brings up bubbling water!
Gushing streams burst forth
When he is near![d]

a 114:2 Or *Judah*, which means praise.
b 114:4 The literal Hebrew states, "mountains skipped like rams, the hills like lambs." This does not mean they skipped with joy, but shook with fear, as the context reveals.
c 114:7 Implied in the text.
d 114:8 Implied in the context.

Psalm 115

THE ONE TRUE GOD

[1]God, glorify your name!
Yes, your name alone be glorified, not ours!
For you are the One who loves us passionately,
And you are faithful and true.
[2]Why should the unbelievers mock us, saying,
"Where is this God of yours?"
[3]But we know our God rules from the heavens
And he does whatever he wants!
[4]The unbelievers worship what they make,
Their wealth and their work.
[5-8]They idolize what they own,
And what they make with their hands,
But their things can't talk to them, or answer their prayers.
Their possessions will never satisfy.
Their futile faith in dead idols and dead works
Can never bring life or meaning to their souls.
Blind men can only create blind things.
Those deaf to God can only make a deaf image.
Dead men can only create dead idols.
And everyone who trusts in these powerless, dead things
Will be just like what they worship—powerless and dead![a]
[9]So trust in the Lord, all his people.
For he is the only true Hero,
The wraparound God who is our Shield!
[10]You, his priests, trust in the Lord.
For he is the only true Hero,
God-wrapped-around-us as our Shield!
[11]Yes, all his lovers who bow before him,

a 115:5–8 Referring to the idols, the literal Hebrew could be translated: "With mouths, but they cannot speak; with eyes, but they cannot see; with ears, but they cannot hear; with noses, but they cannot smell; with hands, but they cannot feel; with feet, but they cannot walk; they cannot talk. Those who make them will become like them, and everyone who trusts in them."

Trust in the Lord.
For he is our only true Hero,
God-wrapped-around-us as our Shield!
12The Lord will never forget us in our need;
He will bless us indeed!
He will bless the house of Israel,
He will bless the house of Aaron, his priest.
13Yes! He will bless his lovers who bow before him,
No matter who they are.
14-15God himself will fill you with more.
Blessings upon blessings will be
Heaped upon you and upon your children,
From the Maker of heaven and earth,
The very God who made you!
16The heavens belong to our God; they are his alone,
But he has given us[a] the earth and put us in charge.
17-18Dead people cannot praise the Lord, but we can!
Those who sink to the silence of the grave
Can no longer give glory to God, but we can!
So let's praise the Lord!
Let's begin now and let it go on until eternity is done.
Hallelujah, and praise the Lord!

a 115:16 Or, "Adam's sons."

Psalm 116

I'M SAVED

[1]I am passionately in love with God
Because he listens to me.
He hears my prayers and answers them.
[2]As long as I live I'll keep praying to him,
For he stoops down to listen to my heart's cry.
[3]Death once stared me in the face, and
I was so close to slipping into its dark shadows.
I was terrified and overcome with sorrow.
[4]I cried out to the Lord,
"God, come and save me!"
[5]He was so kind, so gracious to me.
Because of his passion toward me,
He made everything right and he restored me!
[6]So I've learned from my experience,
That God protects the childlike and humble ones.
For I was broken and brought low,
But he answered me and came to my rescue!
[7]Now I can say to myself and to all:
Relax and rest, be confident and serene,
For the Lord rewards fully
Those who simply trust in him!
[8]God has rescued my soul from death's fear and
Dried my eyes of many tears.
He's kept my feet firmly on his path,
[9]And strengthened me so that I may please him[a]
And live my life before him in his life-giving light!
[10-11]Even when it seems I'm surrounded
By many liars and my own fears,
And though I'm hurting in my suffering and trauma,
I still stay faithful to God and I speak words of faith.

a 116:9 As translated from the Septuagint.

12 So now, what can I ever give back to God
To repay him for the blessings he's poured out on me?
13 I will lift up his cup of salvation
And praise him extravagantly
For all that he's done for me!
14 I will fulfill the promise I made to God
In the presence of his gathered people.
15 When one of God's holy lovers dies,
It is costly to the Lord, touching his heart.
16 Lord, because I am your loving servant
You have broken open my life
And freed me from my chains.
17 Now I'll worship you passionately and bring to you
My sacrifice of praise, drenched with thanksgiving!
18 I'll keep my promise to you, God,
In the presence of your gathered people,
Just like I said I would.
19 I will worship you here in your living presence,
In the temple in Jerusalem.
I will worship and sing "Hallelujah,"
For I praise you, Lord!

Psalm 117

GLORIOUS PRAISE

A praise-psalm

1 Let everyone, everywhere
Shine with praise to Yahweh![a]
Let it all out! Go ahead and praise him!
2 For he has conquered us with his great love,
And his kindness has melted our hearts.
His faithfulness lasts forever,
And he will never fail you.
So go ahead, let it all out!
Praise Yah!
O Yah![b]

a 117:1 The word for *praise* is taken from the word *shine*.
b 117:2 The name *Yah* is not an abbreviated form of *Yahweh*; it is the name of God as he displays his power. *Yahweh* is found 6,830 times in the Hebrew text, and *Yah* is found 49 times.

Psalm 118

GLORIOUS THANKSGIVING

A praise-psalm[a]

[1]Keep on giving your thanks to God,
For he is so good!
His constant, tender love lasts forever!
[2]Let all his princely people sing:
"His constant, tender love lasts forever!"
[3]Let all his holy priests sing:
"His constant, tender love lasts forever!"
[4]Let all his lovers who bow low before him sing:
"His constant, tender love lasts forever!"
[5]Out of my deep anguish and pain I prayed,
And God, you helped me as a Father.
You came to my rescue and broke open the way
Into a beautiful and broad place.
[6]Now I know, Lord, that you are for me, and I will
Never fear what man can do to me.
[7]For you stand beside me as my Hero who rescues me.
I've seen with my own eyes the defeat of my enemies.
I've triumphed over them all!
[8]Lord, it is so much better to trust in you to save me
Than to put my confidence in someone else.
[9]Yes, it is so much better to trust in the Lord to save me
Than to put my confidence in celebrities.
[10]Once I was hemmed in and surrounded by those who don't love you.
But by your supernatural power I overcame them all!
[11-12]Yes, they surrounded me, like a swarm of killer bees,
Swirling around me. I was trapped
Like one trapped by a raging fire;
I was surrounded with no way out and at the point of collapse.

a This is the Psalm or "hymn" that Jesus likely sang after the Passover supper with his disciples, before making his way to Gethsemane and Calvary.

But through your supernatural power I overcame them all!
13They pushed me right up to the edge, and I was ready to fall;
But you helped me to triumph, and together we overcame them all.
14Lord, you are my true strength
And my glory-song,
My Champion, my Savior!
15The joyful songs I now sing will be sung again
In the hearts and homes of all your lovers.
My loud shouts of victory will echo throughout the land.[a]
For my Lord is a Valiant Warrior!
16The power of God is lifted high!
The power of God will never fail!
17You will not let them kill me,
But I will live to tell the world
What the Lord has done for me.
18Yes, the Lord punished me as I deserved,
But he'll never give me over to death.
19Swing wide, you gates of righteousness, and let me pass through,
And I will enter into your presence to worship only you!
20I have found the gateway to God,
The pathway to his presence for all his lovers.
21I will offer all my loving praise to you,
And I thank you so much for answering my prayer,
And bringing me salvation!
22The very stone the masons rejected as flawed,
Has turned out to be the most important capstone of the arch,[b]
Holding up the very house of God.
23The Lord himself is the One who has done this;
And it's so amazing, so marvelous to see!
24This is the very day of the Lord that brings
Gladness and joy, filling our hearts with glee!
25O God, come and save us again; bring us
Your breakthrough-victory!
26Blessed is this One who comes to us,
The Sent-One of the Lord.

a 118:15 Implied in the text.
b 118:22 The words "capstone of the arch" can also be translated "the head of the corner."

And from within the temple we cry: "We bless you!"
27-28For the Lord our God has brought us his glory-light!
I offer him my life in joyous sacrifice.
Tied tightly to your altar I will bring you praise.
For you are the God of my life and I lift you high,
Exalting you to the highest place.
29So let's keep on giving our thanks to God,
For he is so good!
His constant, tender love lasts forever!

Psalm 119

THE WORDS OF GOD[a]

The Way to Happiness

1You're only truly happy when you walk in total integrity;[b]
Walking in the light of God's Word!
2What joy overwhelms everyone who keeps the ways of God,
Those who seek him as their heart's passion!
3They'll never do what's wrong
But will always choose the paths of the Lord.
4God has prescribed the right way to live:
Obeying his laws with all our hearts.
5How I long for my life to bring you glory
As I follow each and every one of your holy precepts!
6Then I'll never be ashamed,
For I take strength from all your commandments.
7I will give my thanks to you from a heart of love and truth.
And every time I learn more of your righteous judgments,
8I will be faithful to all that your Word reveals—
So don't ever give up on me!

True Joy

9How can a young man stay pure?
Only by living in the Word of God and walking in its truth.
10 I have longed for you with the passion of my heart;
Don't let me stray from your directions!
11I consider your prophecies[c] to be my greatest treasure,
And I memorize them and write them on my heart
To keep me from committing sin's treason against you.

a This Psalm is an acrostic poem, a mathematical masterpiece. It consists of twenty-two stanzas of eight lines each. Each stanza begins with the same Hebrew letter at the beginning of every one of its eight lines, going in succession, by strophes, from *alef*—the first letter of the Hebrew alphabet, as the first letter of each line in the first strophe—to *taw*—the last letter of the Hebrew alphabet, as the first letter of each line in the last strophe. Like the eight lines of each stanza there are eight different Hebrew words, all synonyms, used to refer to the Word of God. Although many believe Ezra wrote Psalm 119, the acrostic poetic style is unique to King David within the book of Psalms, which points to his authorship of this Psalm.
b 119:1 Or, "perfection." The Hebrew reads "utterances."
c 119:11 As translated from the Septuagint.

12My wonderful God, you are to be praised above all;
Teach me the power of your decrees!
13I speak continually of your laws
As I recite out loud your counsel to me.
14I find more joy in following what you tell me to do
Than in chasing after all the wealth of the world!
15I set my heart on your precepts
And pay close attention to all your ways.
16My delight is found in all your laws,
And I won't forget to walk in your words.

The Abundant Life

17Let me, your servant, walk in abundance of life,
That I may always live to obey your truth.
18Open my eyes to see the miracle-wonders
Hidden in your Word!
19My life on earth is so brief,
So tutor me in the ways of your wisdom.
20I am continually consumed by these irresistible longings,
These cravings to obey your every commandment!
21Your displeasure rests with those who are arrogant,
Who think they know everything;
You rebuke the rebellious who refuse your laws.
22Don't let them mock and scorn me for obeying you.
23For even if the princes and my leaders choose to criticize me,
I'll continue to serve you and walk in your plans for my life.
24Your commandments are my counselors;
Your Word is my light and delight!

Revived by the Word

25Lord, I'm fading away. I'm discouraged and lying in the dust;
Revive me by your Word, just like you promised you would!
26I've poured out my life before you,
And you've always been there for me,
So now I ask: teach me more of your holy decrees.
27Open up my understanding to the ways of your wisdom,

And I will meditate deeply on your splendor and your wonders.
28My life's strength melts away with grief and sadness;
Come strengthen me, encourage me with your words.
29Keep me far away from what is false;
Give me grace to stay true to your laws.
30I've chosen to obey your truth
And walk in the splendor-light of all that you teach me.
31Lord, don't allow me to make a mess of my life, for I cling to
Your commands and follow them as closely as I can.
32I will run after you with delight in my heart,
For you will make me obedient to your instructions.

Understanding God's Ways

33Give me revelation about the meaning of your ways,
So I can enjoy the reward of following them fully!
34Give me an understanding heart so that I can
Passionately know and obey your truth.
35Guide me into the paths that please you,
For I take delight in all that you say.
36Cause my heart to bow before your words of wisdom
And not to the wealth of this world.
37Help me turn my eyes away from illusions
So that I pursue only that which is true;
Drench my soul with life as I walk in your paths.
38Reassure me of your promises, for I am
Your beloved; your servant who bows before you!
39Defend me from the criticism I face
For keeping your beautiful words.
40See how I long with cravings for more of your ways?
Let your righteousness revive my spirit!

Trust in the Lord

41May your tender love overwhelm me, O Lord,
For you are my Savior and you keep your promises.
42I'll always have an answer for those who mock me
Because I trust in your word.

43May I never forget your truth, for I rely upon your precepts.
44 I will observe your laws every moment of the day,
And will never forget the words you say.
45I will walk with you in complete freedom,
For I seek to follow your every command.
46When I stand before kings I will tell them the truth
And will never be ashamed.
47My passion and delight is in your Word,
For I love what you say to me!
48I long for more revelation of your truth, for I love
The light of your word as I meditate on your decrees.

My Comfort

49Lord, never forget the promises you've made to me,
For they are my hope and confidence.
50In all of my affliction I find great comfort in your promises,
For they have kept me alive!
51No matter how bitterly the proud mockers speak against me,
I refuse to budge from your precepts.
52Your revelation-light is eternal;
I'm encouraged every time I think about your truth!
53Whenever I see the wicked breaking your laws I feel horrible.
54As I journey through life I put all your statutes to music;
They become the theme of my joyous songs.
55Throughout the night I think of you, dear God;
I treasure your every word to me.
56All this joy is mine as I follow your ways!

My Heart is Devoted to You

57You are my Satisfaction, Lord, and all that I need;
So I'm determined to do everything you say.
58With all my heart I seek your favor;
Pour out your grace on me, as you promised!
59When I realize that I'm going astray,
I turn back to obey your instructions.
60I give my all to follow your revelation-light;

I will not delay to obey!
61 Even when temptations encircle me with evil,
I won't forget for a moment to follow your commands.
62 In the middle of night I awake to give thanks to you,
Because of all your revelation-light; so right and true!
63 Anyone who loves you and bows in obedience to your words
Will be my friend.
64 Give me more revelation of your ways,
For I see your love and tender care everywhere.

My True Treasure

65 Your extravagant kindness to me
Makes me want to follow your words even more!
66 Teach me how to make good decisions, and give me
Revelation-light, for I believe in your commands.
67 Before I was humbled I used to always wander astray,
But now I see the wisdom of your words.
68 Everything you do is beautiful, flowing from your goodness;
Teach me the power of your wonderful words!
69 Proud boasters make up lies about me,
Because I am passionate to follow all that you say.
70 Their hearts are dull and void of feelings,
But I find my true treasure in your truth.
71 The punishment you brought me through was the best thing
That could have happened to me, for it taught me your ways.
72 The words you speak to me are worth more
Than all the riches and wealth in the whole world!

Growth Through the Word

73 Your very hands have held me and made me who I am;
Give me more revelation-light so I may learn to please you more.
74 May all your lovers see how you treat me and be glad,
For your words are entwined within my heart!
75 Lord, I know that your judgments are always right,
Even when it's me you judge; you're still faithful and true.
76 Send your kind mercy-kiss to comfort me, your servant,

Just like you promised you would!
77Love me tenderly so I can go on,
For I delight in your life-giving truth.
78Shame upon the proud liars! See how they oppress me,
All because of my passion for your precepts!
79May all your lovers follow me
As I follow the path of your instruction.
80Make me passionate and wholehearted
To fulfill your every wish,
So that I'll never have to be ashamed of myself.

Deliver Me

81I'm lovesick with yearnings for more of your salvation,
For my heart is entwined with your Word.
82I'm consumed with longings for your promises,
So I ask, "When will they all come true?"
83My soul feels dry and shriveled, useless and forgotten,
But I will never forget your living truth.
84How much longer must I wait until you punish my persecutors?
For I am your loving servant.
85Arrogant men who hate your truth and never obey your laws
Have laid a trap for my life.
86They don't know that everything you say is true,
So they harass me with their lies. Help me, Lord!
87They've nearly destroyed my life, but I refuse to yield;
I still live according to your Word.
88Revive me with your tender love and
Spare my life by your kindness, and I'll continue to obey you!

Faith in the Word of God

89Standing firm in the heavens and fastened to eternity,
Is the Word of God.
90Your faithfulness flows from one generation to the next;
All that you created sits firmly in place to testify of you.
91By your decree everything stands at attention,
For all that you have made serves you.

92Because your words are my deepest delight,
I didn't give up when all else was lost.
93I can never forget the profound revelations you've taught me,
For they have kept me alive more than once.
94Lord, I'm all yours, and you are my Savior;
I have sought to live my life pleasing to you.
95Even though evil men wait in ambush to kill me, I will
Set my heart before you, to understand more of your ways.
96I've learned that there is nothing perfect
In this imperfect world, except your words;
For they bring such fantastic freedom into my life!

I Love the Word of God

97O, how I love and treasure the revelation of your word;
Throughout the day I fill my heart with its light!
98By considering your commands
I have an edge over my enemies,
For I take seriously everything you say.
99You have given me more understanding
Than those who teach me,
For I've absorbed your eye-opening revelation.
100You have graced me with more insight than the old sages,
Because I have not failed to walk in the light of your ways.
101I refused to bend my morals when temptation was before me
So that I could become obedient to your word.
102I refuse to turn away from difficult truths,
For you yourself have taught me to love your words.
103How sweet are your living promises to me,
Sweeter than honey is your revelation-light.
104For your truth is the source of my understanding,
Not the falsehoods of those who don't know you, which I despise.

Truth's Shining Light

105Truth's shining light guides me in my choices and decisions;
The revelation of your Word makes my pathway clear.
106To live my life by your righteous rules

Has been my holy and lifelong commitment.
107I'm bruised and broken, overwhelmed by it all;
Breathe life into me again by your living Word.
108Lord, receive my grateful thanks
And teach me more of how to please you.
109Even though my life hangs in the balance,
I'll keep following what you've taught me, no matter what.
110The ungodly have done their best to throw me off track,
But I'll not deviate from what you've told me to do.
111Everything you speak to me is like joyous treasure;
Filling my life with gladness.
112I have determined in my heart to obey whatever you say,
Fully and forever!

Trust and Obey

113I despise those who can't keep commitments,
For I passionately love your revelation-light!
114You're my place of quiet retreat,
And your wrap-around presence
Becomes my shield as I wrap myself in your Word!
115Go away! Leave me, all you workers of wickedness;
For you can't stop me from following every command of my God.
116Lord, strengthen my inner being by the promises of your Word,
So that I may live faithful and unashamed for you.
117Lift me up, and I will be safe. Empower me
To live every moment in the light of your ways.
118Lord, you reject those who reject your laws,
For they fool no one but themselves!
119The wicked are thrown away, discarded and valueless.
That's why I will keep on loving all of your laws!
120My body trembles in holy awe of you, leaving me speechless;
For I'm frightened of your righteous judgments.

I Will Follow Your Ways

121Don't leave me to the mercies of those who hate me,
For I live to do what is just and fair.

122Let me hear your promise of blessing over my life;
Breaking me free from the proud oppressors.
123As a lovesick lover I yearn for more of your salvation
And for your virtuous promises!
124Let me feel your tender love, for I am yours.
Give me more understanding of your wonderful ways.
125I need more revelation from your Word
To know more about you, for I'm in love with you!
126Lord, the time has come for you to break through,
For evil men keep breaking your laws!
127Truly, your message of truth means more to me
Than a vault filled with the purest gold.
128Every word you speak, every truth revealed, is always right
And beautiful to me, for I hate what is phony or false.

I Long to Obey You

129Your marvelous words are living miracles;
No wonder I long to obey everything you say.
130Break open your Word within me
Until revelation-light shines out!
Those with open hearts are given insight into your plans.
131Ineffable cravings and lovesick longings consume me
As I thirst for more revelation of your commands.
132Turn your heart to me, Lord, and show me your grace,
Like you do to every one of your godly lovers.
133Prepare before me a path filled with your promises,
And don't allow even one sin to have dominion over me.
134Rescue me from the oppression of ungodly men,
So that I can keep all your precepts.
135Let your shining face shine brightly on me, your loving servant!
Instruct me on what is right in your eyes.
136When I witness the rebellious breaking your laws
It makes me weep uncontrollably!

His Word is True

137Lord, your judgments reveal your righteousness,
And your verdicts are always fair.

138The motive behind your every word is pure,
And your teachings are remarkably faithful and true.
139I've been consumed with a furious passion to do what's right,
All because of the way my enemies disrespect your laws.
140Every one of your promises has passed the test;
That's why I'm a lover of your Word.
141Even though I'm considered insignificant and despised by the world,
I'll never abandon your ways.
142Your righteousness has no end; it is everlasting,
And your rules are perfectly fair.
143Even though my troubles overwhelm me with anguish,
I still delight and cherish every message you speak to me.
144Give me more revelation so that I can live for you,
For nothing is more pure and eternal than your truth.

Save Me God

145Answer my passionate prayer, O Lord,
And I'll obey everything you say.
146Save me, God, and I'll follow your every instruction.
147Before the day dawns, I'll be crying out for help,
And wrapping your words into my life.
148I lie awake every night pondering your promises to me.
149Lord, listen to my heart's cry,
For I know your love is so real for me;
Breathe life into me again by the revelation of your justice.
150Here they come—these lawless rebels are coming near,
But they are all so far away from your laws.
151God, you are near me always, so close to me;
Every one of your commands reveals truth.
152I've known all along how true and unchanging
Is every word you speak, established forever!

Breathe Life into Me Again

153Look upon all my misery and come be my Hero to rescue me,
For I will never forget what you've revealed to me.
154Take my side and defend me in these sufferings;

Redeem me and revive me, just like you promised you would.
155The wicked are so far from salvation,
For they could not care less about your message of truth.
156Your tender mercies are what I need, O God;
Give me back my life again
Through the revelation of your judgments!
157I have so many enemies who persecute me,
Yet I won't swerve from following your ways.
158I grieve when I see how the faithless ones live,
For they just walk away from your promises.
159Lord, see how much I truly love your instructions,
So in your tender kindness, breathe life into me again.
160The sum total of all your words adds up to absolute truth,
And every one of your righteous decrees is everlasting.

Devoted to God's Word

161The powerful elite have persecuted me without a cause,
But my heart trembles in awe, because of your miracle-words!
162Your promises are the source of my bubbling joy;
The revelation of your Word thrills me,
Like one who has discovered hidden treasure.
163I despise every lie and hate every falsehood,
For I am passionate about keeping your precepts.
164I stop to praise you seven times a day,
All because your ways are perfect!
165There is such a great peace and well-being that comes
To the lovers of your Word, and they'll never be offended.
166Lord, I'm longing for more of your salvation,
For I want to do what pleases you.
167My love for your ways is indescribable;
In my innermost being I want to follow them perfectly!
168I will keep your instructions and follow your counsel;
All my ways are an open book before you.

I Want to Follow You

169 Lord, listen to my prayer. It's like a sacrifice I bring to you;
I must have more revelation of your Word!

170Take my words to heart when I ask you, Lord;
Give me more of your salvation, just like you promised!
171I offer you my joyous praise for all that you've taught me!
172Your wonderful words will become my song of worship,
For everything you've commanded is perfect and true.
173Place your hands of strength and favor upon me,
For I've made my choice to follow your ways.
174I long for more of your salvation, O Lord,
And your words thrill me like nothing else!
175Invigorate my life so that I can praise you even more,
And may your truth be my strength!
176I'll never forget what you've taught me, Lord,
But when I wander off and lose my way,
Come after me, for I am your beloved!

Psalm 120

GOD HELPED ME

A song of the stairway[a]

1I was desperate for you to help me in my struggles,
And you did!
2So come and deliver me now
From this treachery and false accusation.
3O lying deceivers, don't you know what is your fate?
4You will be pierced through with condemnation
And consumed with burning coals of fire!
5Why am I doomed to live as an alien
Scattered among these cruel savages?[b]
Am I destined to dwell in the
Darkened tents of desert nomads?[c]
6For too long I've had to live
Among those who hate peace.
7I speak words of peace,
While they speak words of war,
But they refuse to listen.

a Psalms 120–134 all begin with the words "A song to take you higher" or "A song of ascent" or "A song of the stairway." It is likely these fifteen songs were sung on the fifteen steps that would take the worshipper into the temple. On each step they would stop to worship and sing the corresponding Psalm as they went up higher into the worship of God. Others believe they were the songs sung as David brought up the ark of glory to Jerusalem.

b 120:5 The Hebrew text includes the word *Meshech*, which is a foreign land. The meaning of the word *Meshech* is to scatter, and may refer to ancient Persia.

c 120:5 The Hebrew text includes the word *Kedar*, who was one of Ishmael's sons whose descendants became a wandering group of nomads. *Kedar* means a dark place.

Psalm 121

GOD PROTECTS US

A song of the stairway

1-2 I look up to the mountains and hills,
Longing for God's help.
But then I realize that our true help and protection
Comes only from the Lord,
Our Creator who made the heavens and the earth.
3 He will guard and guide me,
Never letting me stumble or fall.
God is my Keeper;
He will never forget or ignore me.
4 He will never slumber nor sleep;
He is the Guardian-God for his people, Israel.
5 Jehovah himself will watch over you;
He's always at your side to
Shelter you safely in his presence.
6 He's protecting you from all danger
Both day and night.
7 He will keep you from every form of evil or calamity
As he continually watches over you.
8 You will be guarded by God himself.
You will be safe when you leave your home,
And safely you will return.
He will protect you now,
And he'll protect you forevermore!

Psalm 122

JERUSALEM

A song of the stairway by King David[a]

1I was overjoyed when they said:
"Let's go up to the house of the Lord."
2And now at last, we stand here,
Inside the very gates of Jerusalem!
3O Jerusalem, you were built as a city of praise,
Where God and man mingle together.[b]
4This is where all the people of Israel are required
To come and worship Jehovah-God.
5This is where the thrones of kings have been established
To rule in righteousness;
Even King David ruled from here.
6Pray and seek for Jerusalem's peace,
For all who love her will prosper!
7O Jerusalem, may there be peace for those
Who dwell inside your walls,
And prosperity in your every palace.
8I intercede for the sake of my family and friends
Who dwell there, that they may all live in peace!
9For the sake of your house, our God,
I will seek the welfare and prosperity of Jerusalem.

a David wrote this song for the people to sing for the Feasts. It was sung when the worshippers entered the gates of the city, Jerusalem.

b 122:3 The Hebrew phrase "a city bound together" is taken from a root word that means joined, united, coupled. By inference in the context, it is the city where God dwells and man worships.

Psalm 123

A PRAYER FOR MERCY

A song of the stairway

1O God-Enthroned in heaven,
I worship and adore you!
2The way I love you
Is like the way a servant wants to please his master;
The way a maid waits for the orders of her mistress.
We look to you, our God, with passionate longings
To please you and discover more
Of your mercy and grace.
3-4For we've had more than our fill
Of this scoffing and scorn;
This mistreatment by the wealthy elite.
Lord, show us your mercy!
Lord, show us your grace!

Psalm 124

VICTORY

A song of the stairway by King David

1What if God had not been on our side?
Let all Israel admit this!
2-3What if God had not been there for us?
Our enemies, in their violent anger,
Would have swallowed us up alive!
4-5The nations, with their flood of rage,
Would have swept us away
And we would have drowned;
Perished beneath their torrent of terror!
6We can praise God over and over
That he never left us!
God wouldn't allow
The terror of our enemies to defeat us.
7We are free from the hunter's trap;
Their snare is broken and we have escaped!
8For the same God who made everything,
Our Creator and our mighty Maker,
He himself is our Helper and Defender!

Psalm 125

GOD'S SURROUNDING PRESENCE

A song of the stairway

1 Those who trust in the Lord
Are as unshakeable, as unmovable as
Mighty Mount Zion!
2 Just as the mountains surround Jerusalem
So the Lord's wrap-around presence[a]
Surrounds his people,
Protecting them now and forever.
3 The wicked will not always rule over the godly,
Provoking them to do what is evil.
4 God, let your goodness be given away
To your good people;
To all your godly lovers!
5 But those who turn away from truth,
You will turn them away from you,
To follow their crooked ways.
You will give them just what they deserve.[b]
May Israel experience peace
And prosperity!

a 125:2 Implied in the text.
b 125:5 Implied in the text.

Psalm 126

RESTORED

A song of the stairway

[1]It was like a dream come true
When you freed us from our bondage
And brought us back to Zion!
[2]We laughed, and laughed, and overflowed with gladness!
We were left shouting for joy,
And singing your praise.
All the nations saw it and joined in, saying,
"The Lord has done great miracles for them!"
[3]Yes, he did mighty miracles,
And we are overjoyed!
[4]Now, Lord, do it again!
Restore us to our former glory![a]
May streams of your refreshing flow over us,
Until our dry hearts are drenched again.
[5]Those who sow their tears as seeds,[b]
Will reap a harvest with joyful shouts of glee.
[6]They may weep as they go out
Carrying their seed to sow,
But they will return with joyful laughter,
And shouting with gladness as they
Bring back armloads of blessing,
And a harvest overflowing!

a 126:4 Implied in the text.
b 126:5 Or, "sow their seeds with tears." A sower weeps when he sows his precious seed while his children are hungry. This is a picture of sacrificing what little we have for the harvest to come.

Psalm 127

GOD AND HIS GIFTS

A song of the stairway by King Solomon

[1]If God's grace doesn't help the builders,
They will labor in vain to build a house.
If God's mercy doesn't protect the city,
All the sentries will circle it in vain!
[2]It really is senseless to work so hard
From early morning till late at night,
Toiling to make a living
For fear of not having enough.
God can provide for his lovers,
Even while they sleep!
[3]Children are God's love-gift;
They are heaven's generous reward.
[4]Children born to a young couple
Will one day rise to protect
And provide for their parents.[a]
[5]Happy will be the couple
Who has many of them!
A household full of children
Will not bring shame on your name
But victory when you face your enemies,
For your kids will have influence and honor[b]
To prevail on your behalf!

a 127:4 The Hebrew text refers to children as "arrows in the hands of a warrior." This means that children will be our future protection and provision. The more the merrier!
b 127:5 The Hebrew includes a reference to "speaking with your enemies at the gate." This is in the context of children being God's way of blessing parents in their old age.

Psalm 128

THE BLESSINGS OF THE LORD

A song of the stairway

1 How joyous are those who love the Lord
And bow low before God,
Ready to obey him!
2 Your reward will be prosperity,
Happiness, and well-being.
3 Your wife will bless your heart and home.
Your children will bring you joy
As they gather around your table.
4 Yes, this is God's generous reward
For those who love him.
5 May the Lord bless you out of his Zion-glory!
May you see the prosperity of Jerusalem
Throughout your lifetime.
6 And may you be surrounded by your grandchildren.
Happiness to you!
And happiness to Israel!

Psalm 129

PERSECUTED BUT NOT DEFEATED

A song of the stairway

1Let all Israel admit it.
From our very beginning we have been
Persecuted by the nations.
2And from our very beginning,
We have faced never-ending discrimination.
Nevertheless, our enemies have not defeated us.
We're still here!
3They have hurt us more than can be expressed,
Ripping us to shreds, cutting deeply into our souls.
4But no matter what, the Lord is good to us.
He is a righteous God who stood to defend us,
Breaking the chains of the evil ones that bound us!
5May all who hate the Jews
Fall back in disgrace to a shameful defeat!
6Let them be like grass planted in shallow soil
That soon withers with no sustenance.
7Let them be like weeds ignored by the reaper,
And worthless to the harvester.
8Let no one who sees them say,
"May the blessings of Jehovah be upon your life.
May the Lord bless you."[a]

a 129:8 In the Jewish culture, if you passed by one who was harvesting his crops, you would shout out: "The Lord bless you!"

Psalm 130

OUT OF THE DEPTHS

A song of the stairway

1Lord, I cry out to you out of the depths of my despair!
2Hear my voice, O God!
Answer this prayer,
And hear my plea for mercy.
3Lord, if you measured us
And marked us with our sins,
Who would ever have their prayers answered?
4But your forgiving love
Is what makes you so wonderful.
No wonder you are loved and worshipped!
5This is why I wait upon you,
Expecting your breakthrough,
For your word brings me hope.
6I long for you more than any watchman
Would long for the morning light.
I will watch and wait for you, O God,
Throughout the night.
7O Israel, keep hoping, keep trusting,
And keep waiting on the Lord;
For he is tenderhearted, kind, and forgiving.
He has a thousand ways to set you free!
8He himself will redeem you;
He will ransom you from
The cruel slavery of your sins!

Psalm 131

MY HEART IS MEEK

A song of the stairway by King David

1Lord, my heart is meek before you.
I don't consider myself better than others.
I'm content to not pursue matters
That are over my head—
Such as your complex mysteries and wonders—
That I'm not yet ready to understand.
2I am humbled and quieted in your presence.
Like a contented child that rests on its mother's lap,[a]
I'm your resting child,
And my soul is content in you.
3O people of God,[b]
Your time has come to quietly trust,
Waiting upon the Lord,
Now and forever.

a 131:2 "Like a contented child" is literally "like a weaned child."
b 131:3 Or, "O Israel."

Psalm 132

DAVID'S DYNASTY

A song of the stairway

[1]Lord, please don't forget all the hardships
David had to pass through.
[2]And how he promised you,
Jacob's mighty God, saying,
[3]"I will not cross the threshold of my own home
To sleep in my own bed.
[4]I will not sleep or slumber,
Nor even take time to close my eyes in rest,
[5]Until I find a place for you to dwell,
O mighty God of Jacob.
I devote myself to finding a resting place for you!"[a]
[6]The ark first rested at Bethlehem,[b]
Then we found it in the forest of Kiriath-Jearim.
[7]Let's go into God's dwelling place,
And bow down and worship before him.
[8]Arise, O Lord, and enter your resting place,
Both you and the ark of your glorious strength!
[9]May your priests wear the robes of righteousness,
And let all your godly lovers sing for joy!
[10]Don't forsake your anointed king now,
But honor your servant David!
[11]For you gave your word and promised David
In an unbreakable oath that one of his sons
Would be sitting on the throne to succeed him as king.
[12]And you also promised that if David's sons
Would be faithful to keep their promise to follow you,

a 132:5 Historically, this refers to David wanting to bring the ark of alory back to Jerusalem.

b 132:6 Although the Hebrew text does not have the words "ark of glory" but simply "it," the translator supplies the word *ark* from its reference in verse 8. For the sake of understanding the text, the translator has substituted *Ephrathah* for *Bethlehem* (Ephrathah was the ancient name for Bethlehem) and *Jaar* for *Kiriath-Jearim*. (The fields of Jaar was a variant form for Kiriath-Jearim, which means, the city of forests.)

Obeying the words you spoke to them,
Then David's dynasty would never end!
13Lord, you have chosen Zion as your dwelling place,
For your pleasure is fulfilled in making it your home.
14I hear you say, "I will make this place my eternal dwelling,
For I have loved and desired it as my very own!
15I will make Zion prosper and
Satisfy her poor with my provision.
16I will cover my priests with salvation's power,
And all my godly lovers will shout for joy!
17I will increase the anointing that was upon David,
And my glistening glory will rest upon my chosen ones.
18But David's enemies will be covered with shame,
While on them I'll make holiness bloom!"[a]

a 132:18 As translated from the Septuagint. The Hebrew reads, "his crown will sparkle and gleam."

Psalm 133

UNITY

A song to bring you higher by King David

1How truly wonderful and delightful,
To see brothers and sisters living together in sweet unity!
2It's as precious as the sacred scented oil
Flowing from the head of the High Priest, Aaron,
Dripping down upon his beard,
And running all the way down
To the hem of his priestly robes.[a]
3This heavenly harmony can be compared to the dew
Dripping down from the skies upon Mount Hermon,
Refreshing the mountain slopes of Israel.
For from this realm of sweet harmony
God will release his eternal blessing,
The promise of life forever!

a 133:2 Or, "running down the collar of his robe."

Psalm 134

THE NIGHT WATCH

A song to bring you higher

1All his loving priests who serve and sing,
Come and sing your song of blessing to God.
Come and stand before him in the house of God,
Throughout the night watch,
2Lifting up your hands in holy worship;
Come and bless the Lord!
3May the Lord, whom you worship,
The mighty Maker of heaven and earth,
May he bless you from Zion's glory!

Psalm 135

HIS WONDERFUL WORKS

A song to bring you higher

1Shout hallelujah and praise the greatness of God!
All his godly lovers, praise him!
2All you worshipping priests on duty in the temple,
3Praise him, for he is beautiful!
Sing loving praises to his lovely name.
4For Yahweh has chosen Israel for his own purpose,
And we're his special treasure.
5Next to every other god
The greatness of our God is unequaled.
For our God is incomparable!
6He does what he pleases, with unlimited
Power and authority,
Extending his greatness
Throughout the entire universe!
7He forms the misty clouds and creates
Thunder and lightning,
Bringing the wind and rain
Out of his heavenly storehouse.
8He struck down the eldest child in each Egyptian home;
Both men and beast perished that night.
9He did great miracles, mighty signs
And wonders throughout the land,
Before Pharaoh and all his subjects.
10He conquered many nations and
Killed their mighty kings;
11Like Sihon, king of the Amorites,
Also Og, king of Bashan,
And kings from every kingdom in Canaan.
12He gave their land to Israel
As an inheritance for his people.

13O Jehovah, your name endures forever!
Your fame is known in every generation.
14For you will vindicate your persecuted people,
Showing your tender love to all your servants.
15The unbelieving nations worship what they make.
They worship their wealth and their work.
They idolize what they own, and what they do;
16-18 Their possessions will never satisfy.
Their lifeless and futile works
Cannot bring life to them!
Their things' can't talk to them,
Or answer their prayers.
Blind men can only create blind things.
Those deaf to God can only make a deaf image.
Dead men can only create dead idols.
And everyone who trusts in these powerless, dead 'things'
Will be just like what they worship—
Powerless and dead![a]
19Praise Lord-Yahweh, all the families of Israel!
Praise Lord-Yahweh, you family of Aaron![b]
20Let all the priests[c] bless Lord-Yahweh!
Let all His lovers[d] who bow low before him
Praise the Lord-Yahweh!
21So bless the Lord-Yahweh who lives in Jerusalem
And dwells in Zion's glory!
Hallelujah and praise the LORD!

a 135:16-18 Referring to the idols, the Hebrew could be translated, "with mouths, but they cannot speak; with eyes, but they cannot see; with ears, but they cannot hear."
b 135:19 The name Aaron means light-bringer or light-bearer.
c 135:20 Or, "All the family of Levi." Levi represents the holy priesthood.
d 135:20 Or, "those who fear him."

Psalm 136

HIS SAVING LOVE

1Let everyone thank God, for he is good, and he is easy to please!
His tender love for us,
Continues on forever!
2Give thanks to God, our King over all gods!
His tender love for us,
Continues on forever!
3Give thanks to the Lord over all lords!
His tender love for us,
Continues on forever!
4Give thanks to the only miracle working God!
His tender love for us,
Continues on forever!
5Give thanks to the Creator who filled the heavens with revelation!
His tender love for us,
Continues on forever!
6To him who formed dry ground, raising it up from the sea!
His tender love for us,
Continues on forever!
7Praise the One who created every heavenly light!
His tender love for us,
Continues on forever!
8He set the sun in the sky to rule over day!
His tender love for us,
Continues on forever!
9Praise him who set in place the moon and stars to rule over the night!
His tender love for us,
Continues on forever!
10Give thanks to God, who struck down the firstborn in Egypt!
His tender love for us,
Continues on forever!
11He brought his people out of Egypt with miracles!

His tender love for us,
Continues on forever!
12 With his mighty power he brought them out!
His tender love for us,
Continues on forever!
13 He split open the Red Sea for them!
His tender love for us,
Continues on forever!
14 And led his people right through the middle!
His tender love for us,
Continues on forever!
15 He vanquished Pharaoh's armies, drowning them all!
His tender love for us,
Continues on forever!
16 He led his people through the wilderness!
His tender love for us,
Continues on forever!
17 He's the One who smashed mighty kingdoms!
His tender love for us,
Continues on forever!
18 He triumphed over powerful kings who stood in his way!
His tender love for us,
Continues on forever!
19 He conquered Sihon, king of the Amorites!
His tender love for us,
Continues on forever!
20 He conquered the giant named Og, king of Bashan![a]
His tender love for us,
Continues on forever!
21 Then he gave away their lands as an inheritance!
His tender love for us,
Continues on forever!
22 For he handed it all over to Israel, his beloved!
His tender love for us,
Continues on forever!

a 136:20 The name *Og* means giant.

23He's the God who chose us when we were nothing!
His tender love for us,
Continues on forever!
24He has rescued us from the power of our enemies!
His tender love for us,
Continues on forever!
25He provides food for hungry men and animals!
His tender love for us,
Continues on forever!
26Give thanks to the great God of the heavens!
His tender love for us,
Continues on forever!

Psalm 137

THE SONG OF OUR CAPTIVITY

¹Along the banks of Babylon's rivers
We sat as exiles mourning our captivity,
And wept with great love for Zion.
²Our music and mirth were no longer heard, only sadness.[a]
We hung up our harps on the willow trees.
³Our captors tormented us, saying:
"Make music for us and
Sing one of your happy Zion-songs!"
⁴But how could we sing the song of the Lord
In this foreign wilderness?
⁵May my hands never make music again,
If I ever forget you, O Jerusalem;
⁶May I never be able to sing again,
If I fail to honor Jerusalem supremely!
⁷And Lord, may you never forget
What the sons of Edom did to us, saying:
"Let's raze the city of Jerusalem,
And burn it to the ground!"[b]
⁸Listen, O Babylon, you evil destroyer!
The one who destroys you
Will be rewarded above all others!
You will be repaid for what you've done to us.
⁹Great honor will come to those
Who destroy you and your future,
By smashing your infants
Against the rubble of your own destruction.

a 137:2 Implied in the context.
b 137:7 The Hebrew text reads, "strip her [Jerusalem] naked!"

Psalm 138

THE DIVINE PRESENCE

by King David

1I thank you, Lord,
And with all the passion of my heart!
I worship you in the presence of angels,
Heaven's mighty ones will hear my voice
As I sing my loving praise to you!
2I bow down before your divine presence
And bring you my deepest worship,
As I experience your tender love,
And your living truth.
For the promises of your Word
And the fame of your name
Have been magnified above all else!
3At the very moment I called out to you,
You answered me!
You strengthened me deep within my soul,
And breathed fresh courage into me.
4One day all the kings of the earth
Will rise to give you thanks,
When they hear the living words
That I have heard you speak.
5They too will sing of your wonderful ways
For your ineffable glory is so great!
6For though you are lofty and exalted,
You stoop to embrace the lowly.
Yet you keep your distance from those filled with pride.
7Through your mighty power
I can walk through any devastation,
And you will keep me alive, reviving me.
Your power set me free from the hatred of my enemies.
8You keep every promise you've ever made to me!
Since your love for me is so constant and endless,
I ask you, Lord, to finish every good thing that you've begun in me!

Psalm 139

YOU KNOW ALL ABOUT ME

For the Pure and Shining One
King David's poetic song

1Lord, you know everything there is to know about me.
You've examined my innermost being
With your loving gaze.[a]
2You perceive every movement of my heart and soul,
And understand my every thought
Before it even enters my mind.
3-4 You are so intimately aware of me, Lord,
You read my heart like an open book
And you know all the words I'm about to speak
Before I even start a sentence!
You know every step I will take,
Before my journey even begins!
5You've gone into my future to prepare the way,
And in kindness you follow behind me,
To spare me from the harm of my past.
With your hand of love upon my life,
You impart a Father's blessing to me.
6This is just too wonderful,
Deep, and incomprehensible!
Your understanding of me brings me wonder and strength.[b]
7Where could I go from your Spirit?
Where could I run and hide from your face?
8If I go up to heaven, you're there!
If I go down to the realm of the dead, you're there too!
9If I fly with wings into the shining dawn, you're there!
If I fly into the radiant sunset, you're there waiting![c]

a 139:1 Implied in the context. God has discovered everything about you and is intimately and deeply connected to your life.
b 139:6 As translated from the Septuagint. The Hebrew reads, "too high to understand."
c 139:9 Implied in the Hebrew, which states, "the remote parts of the sea," or beyond the horizon to the west. The sea is west of Israel.

10Wherever I go your hand will guide me;
Your strength will empower me.
11It's impossible to disappear from you,
Or to ask the darkness to hide me,
For your presence is everywhere
Bringing light into my night!
12There is no such thing as "darkness" with you.
The night, to you, is as bright as the day;
There's no difference between the two.
13You formed my innermost being,
Shaping my delicate "inside"
And my intricate "outside,"
And wove them all together in my mother's womb.[a]
14I thank you, God, for making me so mysteriously complex!
Everything you do is marvelously breathtaking.
It simply amazes me to think about it!
How thoroughly you know me, Lord!
15You even formed every bone in my body
When you created me in the secret place; [b]
Carefully, skillfully shaping me [c]
From nothing to something.
16You saw who you created me to be,
Before I became me![d]
Before I'd ever seen the light of day,
The number of days you planned for me
Were already recorded in your book.[e]
17-18Every single moment you are thinking of me!
How precious and wonderful to consider,
That you cherish me constantly in your every thought!
O God, your desires toward me are more
Than the grains of sand on every shore!
When I awake each morning

a 139:13 The Hebrew word for *knit*, or *wove* can also be translated "to cover" or "to defend." God places an eternal spirit inside the conceived child within the womb of a mother and covers that life, sends the child a guardian angel, and watches over every child.
b 139:15 The Hebrew text is literally, "the depths of the earth."
c 139:15 Or "embroidered me."
d 139:16 The Hebrew could be translated, "As an embryo."
e 139:16 See Psalm 69:28.

You're still thinking of me.
[19]O God, come and slay these bloodthirsty, murderous men!
For I cry out, "Depart from me, you wicked ones!"
[20]See how they blaspheme your sacred name,
And lift up themselves against you, but all in vain!
[21]Lord, can't you see how I despise those who despise you?
For I grieve when I see them rise up against you.
[22]I have nothing but complete hatred and disgust for them.
Your enemies shall be my enemies!
[23]God, I invite your searching gaze into my heart.
Examine me through and through;
Find out everything
That may be hidden within me.
Put me to the test, and sift through
All my anxious cares.
[24]See if there is any path of pain I'm walking on,
And lead me back to your glorious, everlasting ways,
The path that brings me back to you.

Psalm 140

A PRAYER FOR PROTECTION

For the Pure and Shining One
King David's poetic song

1 Lord, protect me from this evil one!
Rescue me from these violent schemes!
2 He concocts his secret strategy to divide and harm others;
Stirring up trouble, one against another.
3 They are known for their sharp rhetoric of poisonous, hateful words.

Pause in his presence

4 Keep me safe, Lord, out of reach from these wicked and violent men,
And guard me, God, for they have plotted an evil scheme
To ruin me and bring me down.
5 They are proud and insolent; they've set an ambush for me in secret.
They are determined to snare me in their net, like captured prey.

Pause in his presence

6-7 O Lord, you are my God and my saving strength!
My Hero-God, you wrap yourself around me to protect me.
For I'm surrounded by your presence in my day of battle.
Lord Yahweh, hear my cry.
May my voice move your heart to show me mercy.
8 Don't let the wicked triumph over me,
But bring down their every strategy to subdue me,
Or they will become even more arrogant!

Pause in his presence

9 Those who surround me are nothing but proud troublemakers.
May they drink the poison of their own poisonous words.
10-11 May their slanderous lives never prosper!
Let evil itself hunt them down and pursue them relentlessly,
Until they are thrown into fiery pits
From which they will never get out!
Let burning coals of hellfire fall upon their heads!

12 For I know, Lord, that you will be the Hero
Of all those they persecute,
And you will secure justice for the poor.
13 Your godly lovers will thank you no matter what happens.
For they choose and cherish your presence
Above everything else!

Psalm 141

AN EVENING PRAYER

King David's poetic song

1Please, Lord, come close and come quickly to help me!
Listen to my prayer as I call out to you!
2Let my prayer be as the evening sacrifice
That burns like fragrant incense,
Rising as my offering to you
As I lift up my hands in surrendered worship!
3God give me grace to guard my lips[a]
From speaking what is wrong.
4Guide me away from temptation and doing evil.
Save me from sinful habits and from keeping company
With those who are experts in evil.
Help me not to share in their sin in any way!
5When one of your godly lovers corrects me, or one of your faithful ones
Rebukes me, I will accept it like an honor I cannot refuse.
It will be as healing medicine that I swallow without an offended heart.
For even if they are mistaken I will continue to pray.[b]
6When the leaders and judges are condemned,
Falling upon the rocks of justice,[c]
Then they'll know my words to them were true!
7So like an earthquake splits open the earth,
So the world of hell will open its mouth
To swallow their scattered bones.
8But you are my Lord and my God; I only have eyes for you!
I hide myself in you, so don't leave me defenseless.
9Protect me! Keep me from the traps of wickedness they set for me.
10Let them all stumble into their own traps, while I escape
Without a scratch!

a 141:3 The Septuagint reads, "set a fortress door before my lips."
b 141:5 This is one of most difficult verses to translate, with scholars divided over the meaning of the Hebrew text. Another translation could be, "Don't let the oil of the wicked anoint my head, for I pray continually against their wickedness."
c 141:6 See 2 Chronicles 25:12.

Psalm 142

MY ONLY HOPE

King David's poetic song of instruction
A prayer when he was confined in a cave

1God, I'm crying out to you!
I lift up my voice boldly to beg for your mercy!
2I spill out my heart to you,
And tell you all my troubles.
3For when I was desperate, overwhelmed,
And about to give up,
You were the only One there to help.
You gave me a way of escape
From the hidden traps of my enemies.
4I look to my left and right
To see if there is anyone who will help,
But there's no one who takes notice of me.
I have no hope of escape,
And no one cares whether I live or die.
5So I cried out to you, Lord, my only Hiding Place.
You're all I have, my only hope in this life,
My last chance for help.
6Please listen to my heart's cry,
For I am so low and in desperate need of you!
Rescue me from all those who persecute me,
For I am no match for them.
7Bring me out of this dungeon
So I can declare your praise!
And all your godly lovers will celebrate
All the wonderful things you've done for me!

Psalm 143

MY HUMBLE PRAYER

King David's poetic song when he was chased by Absalom[a]

1Lord, you must hear my prayer,
For you are faithful to your promises.
Answer my cry, O righteous God!
2Don't bring me into your courtroom for judgment,
For there is no one who is righteous before you!
3My enemies have chased and caught me,
And crushed my life into dust.
Now I'm living in the darkness of death's shadow.
4My inner being is in depression,
And my heart is heavy, dazed with despair.
5I remember the glorious miracles of days gone by,
And I often think of all the wonders of old.
6Now I'm reaching out to you, thirsting for you
Like the dry, cracked ground thirsts for rain.

Pause in his presence

7Lord, come quickly and answer me,
For my depression deepens and I'm about to give up.
Don't leave me now or I'll die!
8Let the dawning day bring me revelation
Of your tender, unfailing love.
Give me light for my path, and teach me, for I trust in you!
9Save me from all my enemies, for I hide myself in you.
10I just want to obey all you ask of me,
So teach me, Lord, for you are my God.
Your gracious Spirit is all I need, so lead me on good paths
That are pleasing to you, my one and only God!
11Lord, if you rescue me it will bring you more glory,
For you are true to your promises.

a As translated from the Septuagint.

Bring me out of these troubles!
12Since I am your loving servant, destroy all those
Who are trying to harm me.
And because you are so loving and kind to me,
Silence all of my enemies!

Psalm 144

RESCUE ME

King David's poetic song as he stood before Goliath[a]

1There is only one strong, safe, and secure place for me;
It's in God alone, and I love him! He's the One
Who gives me strength and skill for the battle.
2He's my shelter of love and my fortress of faith,
Who wraps himself around me as a secure shield.
I hide myself in this One who subdues enemies before me!
3Lord, what is it about us that you would even notice us?
Why do you even bother with us?
4For man is nothing but a faint whisper, a mere breath.
We spend our days like nothing more than a passing shadow.
5Step down from heaven, Lord, and come down!
Make the mountains melt at your touch.
6Loose your fiery lightning flashes and scatter your enemies.
Overthrow them with your terrifying judgments.
7Reach down from your heavens and rescue me from this hell,
And deliver me from these dark powers.
8They speak nothing but lies; their words are pure deceit.
Nothing they say can ever be trusted.
9My God, I will sing you a brand-new song
When you give me the victory![b]
The harp inside my heart will make music to you!
10I will sing of you, the One who gives victory to kings;
The One who rescues David, your loving servant
From the fatal sword.
11Deliver me, and save me from these dark powers,
Who speak nothing but lies.
Their words are pure deceit;

a As translated from the Septuagint. Put yourself in David's place as he faced a giant named Goliath. Imagine how he felt as you read through this Psalm.
b 144:9 Implied in the text.

And you can't trust anything they say.
12Deliver us! Then our homes will be happy.
Our sons will grow up as strong, sturdy men,
And our daughters with graceful beauty,
Royally fashioned as for a palace.
13-14Our barns will be filled to the brim,
Overflowing with the fruits of our harvest.
Our fields will be full of sheep and cattle,
Too many to count, and our
Livestock will not miscarry their young.
Our enemies will not invade our land,
And there'll be no breach in our walls.
15What bliss we experience when these blessings fall!
The people who love and serve our God
Will be happy indeed!

Psalm 145

GOD'S GREATNESS

King David's poetic song of praise

1My heart explodes with praise to you!
Now and forever my heart bows in worship
To you, my King and my God!
2Every day I will lift up my praise to your name,
With praises that will last throughout eternity.
3Lord, you are great, and worthy of the highest praise!
For there is no end to the discovery
Of the greatness that surrounds you.
4Generation after generation will declare more of your greatness,
And discover more of your glory.[a]
5Your magnificent splendor
And the miracles of your majesty
Are my constant meditation.
6Your awe-inspiring acts of power have everyone talking!
And I'm telling people everywhere about your excellent greatness!
7Our hearts bubble over as we celebrate the fame
Of your marvelous beauty; bringing bliss to our hearts.[b]
We shout with ecstatic joy over your breakthrough for us.
8You're so kind and tenderhearted to those who don't deserve it;
And so very patient with people who fail you.
Your love is like a flooding river overflowing its banks with kindness.
9God, everyone sees your goodness,
For your tender love is blended into everything you do.
10Everything you have made will praise you, fulfilling its purpose.
And all your godly lovers will be found bowing before you!
11They will tell the world of the lavish splendor of your kingdom
And preach about your limitless power.
12They will demonstrate for all to see your miracles of might

a 145:4 Implied in the text.
b 145:7 Implied in the text.

And reveal the glorious majesty of your kingdom.
13You are the Lord that reigns over your never-ending kingdom,
Through all the ages of time and eternity!
You are faithful to fulfill every promise you've made.
You manifest yourself as Kindness in all you do![a]
14Weak and feeble ones, you will sustain.
Those bent over with burdens of shame, you will lift up.
15You have captured our attention, and the eyes of all look to you.
You give what they hunger for, at just the right time!
16When you open your generous hand, it's full of blessings,
Satisfying the longings of every living thing.
17You are right in everything you do;
And your love is wrapped into all your works.
18You draw near to those who call out to you,
Listening ever closely,
Especially when their hearts are true.
19Every one of your godly lovers receives
Even more than what they ask for.
For you hear what their hearts really long for,
And you bring them your saving strength!
20God, you watch carefully over all your lovers
Like a bodyguard;
But you will destroy the ungodly.
21I will praise you, Lord!
Let everyone everywhere join me in praising
The beautiful Lord of holiness,
From now through eternity!

a 145:13 The last two lines of this verse are only found in one reliable Hebrew manuscript and in the Septuagint. It could also be translated, "all your works are very holy."

Psalm 146

OUR TRUE HELP

A poetic psalm by Haggai and Zechariah[a]

1Hallelujah! Praise the Lord!
My innermost being will praise you, Lord!
2I will spend my life praising you and
Singing high praises to you, my God, every day of my life!
3-4We can never look to men for help; no matter who they are
They can't save us,
For even our great leaders fail and fall!
For they too are just mortals who will one day die.
At death the spirits of all depart, and their bodies return to dust.
In the day of their death all their projects and plans are over.
5But those who hope in the Lord
Will be happy and pleased!
Our help comes from the God of Jacob!
6You keep all your promises.
You are the Creator of heaven's glory,
Earth's grandeur, and ocean's greatness.
7The oppressed get justice with you.
The hungry are satisfied with you.
Prisoners find their freedom with you.
8You open the eyes of the blind, and
You fully restore those bent over with shame.
You love those who love and honor you.
9You watch over strangers and immigrants
And support the fatherless and widows.
But you subvert the plans of the ungodly.
10Lord, you will reign forever!
Zion's God will rule throughout time and eternity!
Hallelujah! Praise the Lord!

a As translated from the Septuagint. Psalms 146–150 are called "Hallelujah Psalms" because they all begin in Hebrew with the words "Hallelujah, praise the Lord."

Psalm 147

OUR AMAZING GOD

1 Hallelujah! Praise the Lord!
How beautiful it is when we sing our praises
To the beautiful God;
For praise makes you lovely before him
And brings him great delight!
2 For as we praise him[a]
The Lord builds up Jerusalem,
And gathers up the outcasts, and brings them home!
3 He heals the wounds of every shattered heart.
4 He sets all his stars in place,
Calling them all by their names.
5 How great is our God!
There's absolutely nothing his power cannot accomplish,
And he has infinite understanding of everything.
6 God supports and strengthens the humble,
But the ungodly will be brought down to the dust.
7 Sing out with songs of thanksgiving to the Lord!
Let's sing our praises with melodies overflowing!
8 He fills the sky with clouds, sending showers to water the earth;
So that the grass springs up on the mountain fields,
And the earth produces food for man.[b]
9 All the birds and beasts who cry with hunger to him
Are fed from his hands.
10 His people don't find security in strong horses,[c]
For horse-power is nothing to him.
Man-power is even less impressive!
11 The Lord shows favor to those who fear him;
His godly lovers who wait for his tender embrace.
12 Jerusalem, praise the Lord!

a 147:2 Implied in the context.
b 147:8 As translated from the Septuagint.
c 147:10 Implied in the text.

Zion, worship your God!
13For he has strengthened the authority of your gates.
He even blesses you with more children.
14He's the One who brings peace to your borders,
Feeding you the most excellent of fare.
15He sends out his orders throughout the world;
His words run as swift messengers bringing them to pass.
16He blankets the earth with glistening snow,
Painting the landscape with frost.
17Sleet and hail fall from the sky,
Causing waters to freeze before winter's icy blast.
18Then he speaks his word and it all melts away;
As the warm spring winds blow, the streams begin to flow.
19In the same way he speaks to his people and to Israel,
Bringing them his life-giving words.
20He has dealt with Israel
Differently than with any other people,
For they have received his laws.
Hallelujah! Praise the Lord!

Psalm 148

THE COSMIC CHORUS OF PRAISE

1Hallelujah! Praise the Lord!
Let the skies be filled with praise,
And the highest heavens with the shouts of glory!
2Go ahead—praise him, all you his messengers!
Praise him some more, all you heavenly hosts!
3Keep it up—sun and moon!
Don't stop now, all you twinkling stars of light!
4Take it up even higher—up to the highest heavens,
Until the cosmic chorus thunders his praise![a]
5Let the entire universe erupt with praise to God.
From nothing to something he spoke, and created it all.
6He established the cosmos to last forever,
And he stands behind his commands,
So his orders will never be revoked.
7Let the earth join in with this parade of praise!
You mighty creatures of the ocean's depths, echo in exaltation!
8Lightning, hail, snow, and clouds,
And the stormy winds that fulfill his word.
9Bring your melody, O mountains and hills,
Trees of the forest and field, harmonize your praise!
10-12Praise him all beasts and birds, mice and men,
Kings, Queens, princes, and princesses,
Young men and maidens, children and babes,
Old and young alike, everyone everywhere!
13Let them all join in with this orchestra of praise.
For the name of the Lord is the only name we raise!
His stunning splendor ascends higher than the heavens.
14He anoints his people with strength and authority,
Showing his great favor to all his godly lovers,
Even to his princely people, Israel, who are so close to his heart.
Hallelujah! Praise the Lord!

a 148:4 Poetic implication in the text. The literal Hebrew reads, "the waters above the sky."

Psalm 149

TRIUMPHANT PRAISE

1Hallelujah! Praise the Lord!
It's time to sing to God a brand-new song,
So that all his holy people will then hear
How wonderful he is!
2May Israel be enthused with joy all because of him,
And may the sons of Zion pour out
Their joyful praises to their King.
3Break forth with dancing!
Make music and sing God's praises
With the rhythm of drums!
4For he enjoys his faithful lovers.
He adorns the humble with his beauty,
And he loves to give them the victory.
5His godly lovers triumph in the glory of God,
And their joyful praises will rise even while others sleep.
6God's high and holy praises fill their mouths,
For their shouted praises are their weapons of war!
7These warring weapons will bring vengeance
On every opposing force and every resistant power,
8To bind kings with chains and rulers with iron shackles.
9Praise-filled warriors will enforce
The judgment-doom decreed against their enemies.
This is the glorious honor he gives to
All his godly lovers.
Hallelujah! Praise the Lord!

Psalm 150

THE HALLELUJAH CHORUS

1Hallelujah! Praise the Lord!
Praise God in his holy sanctuary!
Praise him in his stronghold in the sky!
2Praise him for his miracles of might!
Praise him for his magnificent greatness!
3Praise him with the trumpets blasting!
Praise him with piano and guitar!
4–5Praise him with drums and dancing!
Praise him with the loud, resounding clash of cymbals!
Praise him with every instrument you can find!
6Let everyone everywhere join in
The crescendo of ecstatic praise to Yahweh!
Hallelujah! Praise the Lord!

About the Translator

Dr. Brian Simmons is known as a passionate lover of God. After a dramatic conversion to Christ, Brian knew that God was calling him to go to the unreached people of the world and present the gospel of God's grace to all who would listen. With his wife Candice and their three children, he spent nearly eight years in the tropical rain forest of the Darien Province of Panama as a church planter, translator, and consultant. Brian was involved in the Paya-Kuna New Testament translation project. He studied linguistics and Bible translation principles with New Tribes Mission. After their ministry in the jungle, Brian was instrumental in planting a thriving church in New England (U.S.), and now travels full time as a speaker and Bible teacher. He has been happily married to Candice for over forty-two years and is known to boast regularly of his children and grandchildren. Brian and Candice may be contacted at:

brian@passiontranslation.com
Facebook.com/passiontranslation
Twitter.com/tPtBible

For more information about the translation project or any of Brian's books, please visit:

www.thepassiontranslation.com
www.stairwayministries.org